The Trading Playbook

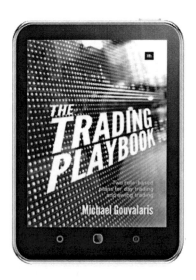

The Trading Playbook

Two rule-based plans for day trading and swing trading

By Michael Gouvalaris

HARRIMAN HOUSE LTD

18 College Street

Petersfield

Hampshire

GU31 4AD

GREAT BRITAIN

Tel: +44 (0)1730 233870

Email: contact@harriman-house.com

Website: www.harriman-house.com

First published in Great Britain in 2015

Paperback ISBN: 9780857194596

eBook ISBN: 9780857194763

British Library Cataloguing in Publication Data

A CIP catalogue record for this book can be obtained from the British Library.

Contents

About the author

Michael Gouvalaris is an Investment Advisor Representative at James D. Maxon Financial Advisors. He is also an active contributor to investing. com and runs his own website, theTechnicalInvestor.wordpress.com. On the Technical Investor he offers market analysis and performance measures of a variety of different asset classes.

Michael can be contacted at tradingplaybook2014@gmail.com.

Disclaimer

This book was created for educational purposes only. All opinions and analysis expressed in the book are for educational and entertainment purposes only, and are not guaranteed in any way. In no event shall this book or anyone involved with it have any liability for any losses incurred in connection with any decision made, whether action or inaction, based upon the information provided in this book.

Nothing in this book should be taken as investment advice. Trading and investing is very risky, please consult your personal investment advisor before making any investment decisions.

Trading Playbook Live

The Trading Playbook doesn't end with the book you're reading now. With my **Trading Playbook Live** service, you can keep up to date with my ongoing analysis and follow what I am doing as I analyse promising trade setups in real-time.

My plan is to issue from three to five live updates a month by email, with each update containing an analysis of real-time trading setups in global markets. I will cover a range of markets for different assets, and I will invite readers to submit their requests for areas they would like me to analyse.

As you receive my updates, you will see the trading techniques I discuss in the *Trading Playbook* come to life.

Visit **www.harriman-house.com/tradingplaybook** or email **contact@harriman-house.com** for more information and to sign up for **Trading Playbook Live**.

Preface

What this book covers

There are generally two types of traders. You have **day traders** who are looking to get in and out of the market in the same day, often multiple times. Day traders look at intraday charts. Then you have **swing traders**. They generally hold positions for days, weeks and even months and they look at longer-term charts. Whichever of these two methods most closely fits your trading style, there is something in *The Trading Playbook* for you.

The first section of the playbook presents a simple and highly effective day trading system that quantifies ten different daily scenarios by certain characteristics that develop in real time. Between these ten different **day types**, every possible market scenario is captured. I outline high probability and low probability outcomes based upon what day type is in progress. I call this the *day trading playbook*.

Next, there is a section on swing trading. Here, I detail effective ways to identify the trend, how to find ideal spots to enter trades in the direction of the trend, and also how to identify signals that warn of potential trend failure or reversals. You will learn simple and highly effective tools for spotting high probability entries and exits for trades. This is the *swing trading playbook*.

The key benefits of the playbooks are that they give traders a well-defined plan to follow. This alleviates many of the big mistakes traders face, such as over-trading, cutting winners too early, or sitting in losing trades too long. Such actions create the opportunity for devastating losses. Many traders I have talked with over the years have no solid plan, so their trading is akin to gambling or excessive speculation.

In the course of the book, I will also discuss risk management and a few additional tips that helped me in my trading – I know they can help you too.

All the material is geared towards simplicity and effectiveness. It is designed to help traders refine their approach and to give them additional tools to assist in their market analysis and trade placement. It is suitable for those who have some experience in reading price charts and are familiar with the basic terms and concepts of trading. If you are new to trading, I recommend you start with a beginner's guide first.

Markets, time frames and software

The day trading playbook targets the futures market – specifically the E-mini S&P 500 futures (ES). The E-mini S&P 500 is the world's most actively traded futures market, with over 2.2 million contracts traded on an average day. This extremely liquid market is very helpful as support and resistance tends to work better with higher volumes and it helps ensure order fills with very little, if any, slippage.

The day trading playbook is effective in other futures markets, such as oil, the euro, etc., but they have slightly different trading hours – or pit sessions – that you would have to be aware of. Also, because many futures markets are much less liquid than the S&P 500 futures, there is the heightened probability that prices can overshoot key support or resistance levels, so stops would need to be adjusted accordingly to account for the increased volatility.

The swing trading playbook works with any market or investment vehicle, whether that be stocks, ETFs, futures, etc.

The day trading playbook recommends that trades be placed during the regular trading hours session (so for the ES futures this is 9:30am to 4:15pm EST). Trading during off hours gives no edge in the short term, so it's no better than gambling.

The swing trading playbook has no preferential time frames; trades can be placed at any time.

There is no special software or equipment required to follow any of my trading plan. All you need is a basic charting software package able to receive intraday market data. This is provided by just about any reliable futures broker and investment platform.

The playbook

After some thought, I decided to call this *The Trading Playbook*; drawing a comparison to the playbook that an NFL (American National Football League) team might use. One characteristic all great NFL players and coaches share is their dedication to studying tapes of games over many hours. That same type of dedication is required to become successful in trading.

A quarterback studies videos of games to see the opposing teams' tendencies. He looks to see different formations, what directions the opponent blitzes from, and many other elements. As traders, we study price charts to find different tendencies and patterns the market leaves behind so that we can take advantage of these the next time.

Of course, no two market days will be exactly alike; however, I do believe each day leaves behind certain characteristics that can give us an edge. In this book I will highlight many of these characteristics in a simple and effective format.

My trading journey

I began trading in 2008, when you could seemingly short anything and make money. At a basic level it appeared as if I was having success, but I didn't have a solid plan or strategy. My early wins led to overconfidence, which eventually led to taking some large losses. I'm not going to lie, the losses hurt, especially at a time when the economy was tanking and every dollar mattered. But the losses were a valuable lesson for me, as they brought me to the point where I made a firm commitment to come up with a solid plan if I was to ever risk another dollar trading. Yes, my days of just placing random orders on a whim were over.

The journey wasn't easy, nothing good in life is. My first inclination was to seek complication. This consisted of trying every indicator under the sun, usually five or six at a time, for surely the more complex the setup of indicators, the greater the odds of success when a signal is delivered, right? Unfortunately, that part of the journey never produced any real fruit for me. I'm sure some people can use indicators with success, but I found they always lagged price. By the time I got the *signal*, most if not all of the trading opportunity had already taken place.

Maybe you've been there; maybe you're currently experiencing the same levels of frustration and looking for a solution. I'm going to share with you what worked for me in a simple and effective format. When I chose simplicity over complexity I began to improve my trading performance. I focused on *price action only* and that was the beginning of my turnaround.

The second and equally important concept that helped improve my trading performance was to begin thinking in terms of probabilities. This gave me focus and direction for each day, and also kept me from becoming wedded to one side of the trend and getting run over if I was wrong. It then became much easier to quickly exit a losing trade early and admit defeat, moving on to the next opportunity. Before, I would hold on and hope I could just get out and break even, usually resulting in catastrophe. That was not a sound strategy.

The third and final element was hard work and screen time – watching the market move and studying the patterns it left behind. It took some time to figure out what to look for, but after a while it started to come together and make sense.

To summarise, the three foundations of the trading method in the playbook are:

1. Simplicity over complexity.

2. Think in terms of probabilities.

3. Hard work and screen time.

A simple and effective blueprint

Now, I don't want to give the wrong impression, this is not a get-rich-quick scheme. As I said before, we need to think in terms of probabilities as traders. If certainty is what you seek, the stock market is not the place you should be looking. However, I firmly believe this simple and effective system can give you a blueprint and a guide to improve your trading performance.

One of my favourite quotes is from Mark Twain:

"History never repeats itself, but it often rhymes."

As I was developing my trading approach, it occurred to me that you can substitute the word *history* in this quote with *markets*. Obviously, no two trading days are ever completely harmonious. But there are enough characteristics left behind each day to form a simple and effective trading strategy.

So, without further ado, let's dive into the material. Our first task is to consider risk management and then we will move on to the two playbooks.

Risk Management

Risk management, or money management, is the single most important concept in trading. Traders, especially those new to the game, spend too much time searching for the perfect trading system and not enough on their personal risk management strategy. There is not a system, indicator or methodology out there that is anywhere close to 100%. The goal should not be perfection, but focusing on a system that fits your style and produces more wins than losses. Then, with a sound money management strategy, the trading account will grow over time.

Everyone's personal risk tolerance is different, according to their trading style. A scalper may maximise their margin and leverage in short trades only looking for ticks, in which case the stop loss wouldn't be too far away. A swing trader would be targeting an expected return of multiple points, so in turn their stop would be further away from the entry point.

There is no one-size-fits-all with anything regarding trading. Personally, I try to achieve as close to a 1-to-2 risk-to-reward ratio as I possibly can for each trade – you will notice I refer to this a number of times in the playbook. If I cannot achieve a 1-to-2 risk-to-reward ratio, or close to it, then I will not take the trade.

Calculating a risk-to-reward ratio

Calculating a risk-to-reward ratio is very easy. You divide the total gross profit potential by the maximum dollar amount you are comfortable risking.

Let's say you see a good long trade setup on the S&P 500 futures (ES) that has a target that is 5 points away and a support level only one point below. You decide to place a stop two points below entry to allow for some short-term volatility.

In this equation, your total gross profit would be $250 ($50 a point x 5 points) and the total amount you are risking would be $100 ($50 a point x 2 points). In this case your risk-to-reward ratio would equal 2.5-to-1 ($250 divided by $100). This is a favourable ratio to go ahead and take the trade.

Many successful traders will not take a trade with a risk-to-reward ratio below 2. This makes sense as a risk-to-reward ratio below 2 would need a very high win-rate to stay profitable. On the other hand, let's look at the benefits of a 1-to-2 risk-to-reward ratio for your long-term trading profit.

Benefits of a 1-to-2 risk-to-reward ratio

Using a simple example to illustrate, let's take the ES (E-mini S&P 500 futures) and risk $50 per contract to make $100 per contract. After ten trades, with a 50% win rate you would be up $250 overall. A 40% win rate after ten trades would result in you being up $100 overall. It's not until you hit a win rate of below 35% that your account starts to experience drawdowns. Do keep in mind that this example does not take account of commissions.

The results after 100 trades with a 1-to-2 risk-to-reward ratio are displayed in Figure 1.

Figure 1: 100 trades with a 1-2 risk-to-reward ratio

	50% win rate	40% win rate	35% win rate
Gain	$5000	$4000	$3500
Loss	-$2500	-$3000	-$3250
Total	$2500	$1000	$250

My goal here is to show you how good money management skills can help total returns over time. With the tools and the probabilities of each day type that are outlined in the playbook, I firmly believe you can achieve and even exceed the win rates above.

Regression of daily volatility

An area I need to address as part of risk management is the regression of daily volatility. In the recent past it was common to see intraday movements in the indices of around 3% to 5%. More recently, it's become almost a big deal if there is a 0.50% move in the major averages in a single day.

It is clear that the regression of intraday volatility is not good for traders. Let's say you're looking to target a 1-to-2 risk-to-reward ratio while trading for targets that are 5 or more ES points away. With an Average True Range (ATR) of 8 points (as it is for the S&P 500 futures at the time of writing), then the reality is that it may be unrealistic for you to target a 5 point move, as you are needing to almost capture the top and bottom tick of the day in this move. A way to get around this would be to increase your position size and lower your targets. So instead of trading one contract looking for 5 points while risking 2 points, you would trade 2 contracts looking for 2.5 points and risking 1 point.

The challenge of controlling emotions

Such a trade is a test of the trader's emotions. Let's say your profit target is 2 points away. What often happens is price gets close to your profit target and then pulls back to your entry. You go from being ecstatic that your target looks like it will get hit, to being deflated that you are now back to break even. You think to yourself, "Why is this happening to me?"

Then you become fearful that this once promising trade is not only going to yield zero, but may very well cost you by taking out your stop loss and proving to be a losing trade. You see the price tick up one tick above entry and in a mad dash of emotions you say to yourself, "I can close this trade out now with a small gain rather than take the loss," and in the heat of the moment you hit the sell button for a one tick or one quarter point profit, only to see the price race higher to where your profit target would have been. This is why you must learn to control your emotions as a trader – if you are struggling to keep control in such situations then I would advocate closing all positions and stepping away from the trading screen for a while.

Trading multiple lots and scaling out

One way to counter regression of volatility is to trade multiple lots at once and take profits as the trade proceeds – also referred to as scaling out. When doing this, the trader is able to reduce and possibly even eliminate the risk in a trade, thereby maintaining a cool head and being able to let the remaining position continue to its perceived target.

For those trading multiple lots and wanting to use a scale out technique, there are a variety of different methods at your disposal. One approach is to get into the trade a couple of ticks ahead of a key price area, then move your stop to break even for part of your lot and let the rest of the lot run. What I mean by this is as follows.

Say you have a limit order in place at 1900 and you want to enter a short trade at that point. In order for the limit order to get filled you would need the price to trade through 1900, so if you want to buy 1900 you would actually need 1899.75 to trade (one tick below 1900 on the S&P 500 futures) before you get filled. Instead you may wish to set your limit order a couple of ticks above 1900, say at 1900.50, to ensure that you get filled as the price approaches 1900. If it is an important level, there may be other traders waiting to buy that level as well, creating excessive demand that may mean the price doesn't drop low enough to fill an order that has been left right at 1900.

Once in the trade, you can scale out after a couple of ticks and move your stop up to break even. I know some successful traders who will scale out and take some profits after 2 to 3 ticks on the ES, just for psychological reasons and to get a good head start. This is not a bad idea, especially if you're going through a rough patch in your trading. Just getting any target hit, even for a couple ticks, can be refreshing after a series of tough defeats.

Think about what works best for you

I encourage you to work with some possible outcomes in an Excel spreadsheet or using a risk-reward calculator (you can find these with a Google search) and come up with a good plan that works for you.

Some traders like the all in, all out approach for its simplicity and maximum profit potential. Others prefer the scaling out technique to calm emotions and take what the market gives them. There is no right or wrong answer, but quantifying your ideas and having a full understanding of your risk-to-reward strategies will go a long way to keeping you disciplined and focused.

With risk management covered, let's now move on to the playbooks.

Day Trading Playbook

INTRODUCTION

Day trading is a process where you attempt to profit from the short-term fluctuations in prices within a given day, generally exiting all positions before the close of the day. Day traders have the odds stacked against them as they have to deal with the psychological issues that affect investors and swing traders – greed and fear – but to a much greater extent and more often.

I have geared the day trading playbook towards the futures market, specifically the ES, or E-mini S&P 500 futures contracts. This is the most popular futures market, with the highest volume and liquidity. The futures market tends to be where most serious traders reside as the tax efficiency, all day tradability and margin capabilities are more favourable.

However, even though I focus on the E-mini S&P 500, the principles presented can still be applied to other futures markets, like the euro and oil, and even stocks and ETFs. The regular trading hours may have to be adjusted accordingly for certain vehicles like the euro futures contract, and the expectations may have to be adjusted for highly volatile vehicles like oil futures or less liquid stocks, but the basic principles remain the same.

Since day traders have the odds stacked against them, it is imperative for anyone attempting to day trade to create a plan and stick with it. While it may be true that much of day trading is pure speculation – after all there are no certainties in financial markets – the first step is to break things down and think in terms of probabilities instead of certainties. The next step is to formulate a well-defined plan in terms of execution and expectations.

In the day trading playbook I have laid out a well-defined plan that is simple to learn and follow. I have created a few basic characteristics of the trading day and these form ten different day setups that cover every possible scenario you will encounter. These day scenarios outline what the trader's expectations for the day should be and what trade setups to look for. Under my rules, trades are placed during the regular trading session hours only, but I do observe after-market indicators like the overnight high and overnight low.

Alongside my own rules, I describe how I use measures of volatility, support and resistance, and inside days to aid my analysis and trade placement.

I will present real examples for each of the ten days along with a bullet point list of guidelines to help you make successful trading decisions.

So let's begin.

THE STRUCTURE OF A MARKET DAY

There are three elements that make up each day in the market:

1. Day type
2. Gap type
3. Open type

Based upon these three elements, there are ten different combinations that make up the trading playbook. The first element to look at is **day type**.

1. Day type

In order to define what day type we are seeing, we need to use the data from the pit session or regular trading hours (RTH) only. The reason for this is that the RTH session is generally when the most volume occurs.

As stated above, my trading principles can apply to any market with good trading volumes and liquidity. The market I focus on is the E-mini S&P 500 futures contracts (ES). So, in this case, the regular trading hours session would be from the 9:30am EST open to the 4:15pm EST close.

There are three day types:

Up day

A trading day that concludes with the closing price ending **higher** than where it opened at 9:30am EST. Figure 2 shows an example of an up day.

Figure 2: Up day

Down day

A trading day that concludes with the closing price ending **lower** than where it opened at 9:30am EST. Figure 3 shows an example of a down day.

Figure 3: Down day

Neutral day

A trading day that concludes with the closing price ending **equal to** where it opened at 9:30am EST. (This day type is rare – I will discuss how to deal with this scenario in further detail later in the book.) Figure 4 shows an example of a neutral day.

Figure 4: Neutral day

It's important to note that we are not concerned whether the market closed positive or negative for the day. That is not what I am talking about when referring to up days or down days. We are only concerned with how the market closed in relation to its open.

For example, the market could gap up 1% on the previous day's close, but close up only 0.5% on the previous day's close. In this case, the market closed lower than where it opened the session. It resulted in a down day type, even though the market as a whole closed in positive territory. This is a subtle yet distinct aspect of my method.

Don't worry, in the end I will put it all together so it makes sense. For now, I just want to get you familiar with each of the concepts individually.

The next element that comprises the trading day is the **gap type**.

2. Gap type

Like the day type, this concept is straightforward.

One of the features of the futures markets is their all-day tradability, as opposed to stocks and options which only trade during the regular trading hours of the market. The after-hours session is called the Globex or overnight session, and the volume is generally much lighter.

This low volume is one of the reasons why my system doesn't allow for any trading during off hours – the market can be even more unpredictable during these periods and I don't see any statistical edge in placing trades at this time. The six and a half hours during the regular trading hours session is more than enough time to find some high probability opportunities.

During these off hours, economic news, macro headline events, global markets and other factors can affect the futures markets, and cause them to open higher or lower than where they settled the previous day. Where the market opens in proportion to its prior day closing price is called the gap.

I will now describe the three gap types.

Gap up

When the 9:30am EST opening print is **higher** than the previous trading day's closing price. Figure 5 shows an example of a gap up.

Figure 5: Gap up

Gap down

When the 9:30am EST opening print is **lower** than the previous trading day's closing price. Figure 6 shows an example of a gap down.

Figure 6: Gap down

Unchanged gap

When the 9:30am EST opening print is **equal to** the previous day's closing price. (Like the neutral day type, a neutral gap type is rare. I will provide additional notes on this later.) Figure 7 shows an unchanged gap.

Figure 7: Unchanged gap

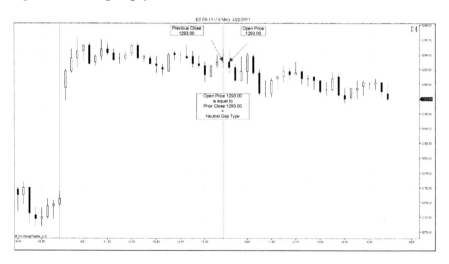

3. Open type

The last element of the trading day is the **open type**. An open type essentially means where the market opened compared to the previous trading day (also referred to as the trading session).

There are a couple of simple concepts to understand as part of the way I look at the open type.

The first concept is the *range*. We are going to think in terms of the entire trading range for the previous day. So if the ES traded with a low of 1900 and a high of 1910, the entire trading range for that day would be 1900-1910.

The next concept is the *previous day's open price*; this is where the actual pit session for the previous day began trading. Some market profilers look at the first swing high to low off the open on a 1 minute or tick chart. Personally, I tend to keep it simple and look at the open price for the very first price bar at 9:30am EST on that day.

So, bearing in mind these concepts, let's now look at the four basic open types.

Above range/above previous day's open

When the market opens **above** the previous trading day's high, and also **above** the previous day's open price. An example is shown in Figure 8.

Figure 8: Above range/above previous day's open

In range/above previous day's open

When the market opens **inside** the previous day's trading range, and also **above** the previous day's open price. An example is shown in Figure 9.

Figure 9: In range/above previous day's open

In range/below previous day's open

When the market opens **inside** the previous day's trading range and **below** the previous day's open. An example is shown in Figure 10.

Figure 10: In range/below previous day's open

Below range/below previous day's open

When the market opens **below** the previous trading day's low of the day, and also **below** the open price of the previous trading day. An example is shown in Figure 11.

Figure 11: Below range/below previous day's open

When we identify open types, it will become very important to be aware of the midpoint of the prior trading day. This will come into play in determining the probable outcomes, as I will discuss in greater detail later.

Most charting packages come with a Fibonacci retracement tool. You can easily find the midpoint of the trading day by selecting the high and dragging it down to the low (or vice versa) to calculate the 50% line. Another way to calculate the midpoint is to add the high of the day to the low of the day and divide by two. An example of finding the midpoint using the Fibonacci retracement tool is given in Figure 12.

Figure 12: Using the Fibonacci retracement tool to find the midpoint of the trading day

MEASURING MARKET VOLATILITY

You will find it useful to have an awareness of market volatility, or the market's daily price fluctuation potential. Knowing how far the market has moved on recent days and how far it is likely to move today will help you to better define specific price levels to trade from and targets to aim for. The two volatility tools that I have found to work the best are:

1. Average True Range.
2. Volatility Index.

Average True Range

Average True Range (ATR) is a measure of volatility introduced by J. Welles Wilder in his book, *New Concepts in Technical Trading Systems*. The indicator is displayed as a moving average of the true ranges, with the average typically taken over the last 14 days.

A higher ATR reading generally means a higher level of volatility. A lower ATR reading generally means a lower level of volatility.

In general terms, over the last ten years an ATR reading above 20 on the S&P 500 is an above average level of volatility. However, in 2008 the ATR readings got into the 70s and during the 2010 flash crash and the 2011 euro crisis periods ATR hit the 40s. So the 20 threshold is by no means a definite indicator, but rather it is a gauge of the recent level of volatility to add into your risk-reward analysis.

For example, if ATR levels have been around 25 in the recent action, which is slightly above average, that is a signal to add some extra distance between your entry and your stop level. This may mean that you must trade in a smaller size or look for opportunities where the potential target would yield a higher than average return to compensate for the extra risk. These adjustments are extremely important to make when volatility rises and decreases.

Conversely, over the last 15 years the average low ATR reading on the S&P 500 is 10. It's hit that number a significant amount of times in the last couple years and never really gets much lower. This generally represents a lack of volatility (or complacency), which is in most cases bullish for stocks.

The ATR indicator is available on most charting applications. Figure 13 shows an example of a price chart with the ATR included below it.

Figure 13: ATR chart

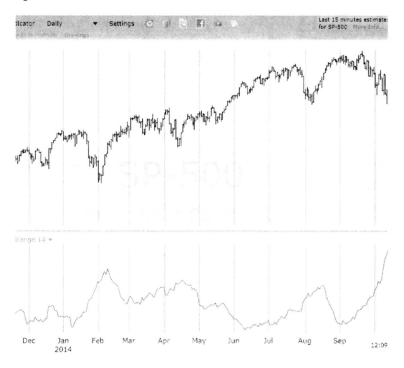

You generally want to look at ATR from a daily perspective. In other words, you want to find the Average True Range for each trading day, not the Average True Range for each 15 minute bar. You can easily calculate this yourself, but it's even easier to let the computer do the math for you.

Why is this important and how does it tie into the playbook?

Understanding the ATR reading for the vehicle that you are trading is an important piece of the puzzle because it gives you an idea of how far price may travel in a certain direction on any given day.

For instance, let's say the ATR on the S&P 500 has been at 10, and on this particular day price has rallied about 8 points from its low. This information is telling you that since the average range has been 10 and we have already experienced an 8 point move in this session, entering a momentum trade in the direction of the trend today does not have a great probability of success. In fact, a counter trend trade may be more beneficial.

Another example may be if we have an ATR of 10 while today's price has only rallied 5 points off its low. In this example, since we still have another 5 points before we hit the average range, a trade in the direction of the prevailing trend has a greater probability of success.

Volatility Index (VIX)

You can also use the **Volatility Index (VIX)** to help calculate average daily fluctuation potential. Most people will recognise the VIX as a pricing model for options, as well as a gauge of fear in the markets. While this is true, there is also another use for the VIX that very few people seem to know about. We can calculate the average daily fluctuation by using a formula that includes the current reading of the VIX. The formula takes the current value of the VIX divided by the square root of the number of days in a year (which is 19.1) and applies this to the S&P 500 to get a percentage value:

average daily fluctuation = (S&P price x (VIX / 19.1))/100

For example, as I write this, the VIX currently resides at 11.50 and the S&P 500 is trading around 1960. If you take that 11.50 and divide it by 19.10 (square root of the number of days in a year) you get approximately 0.60%. This means the average daily fluctuation is around 11.76 points (0.60% of S&P 500 at 1960).

Traders use this figure in the same way as the ATR – if the average daily fluctuation is 11.76 points and today's action has already seen a move of 10 points, the probability is that it doesn't have much further to go. And vice versa – if there has only been a 2 point move so far in today's session and the average daily fluctuation is 11.76, then there could be a further move to come.

Both ATR and VIX basically arrive at the same conclusion and they can both provide you with extra information to help you with your market analysis. While there are always macro events such as central bank policy changes, earnings reports, extreme weather, etc., that act as catalysts for above average daily ranges, as traders the goal is to focus on the probabilities, our edge and what is realistic, otherwise you are dealing in pure speculation.

SUPPORT AND RESISTANCE

Every trader uses support and resistance in some shape or form. It's how one goes about identifying what is support and what is resistance that differs.

In my search for simplicity, I use only prior swing highs and lows and open price gaps as support and resistance areas. I find that, like having too many indicators on the screen, identifying too many forms of support and resistance will lead to you having a key level every few points. That can end up becoming more confusing than helpful.

You can identify these levels on any time frame. So if you're a day trader, you may use the 30 to 60 minute charts to identify levels and then switch to your 5 minute chart to trade. If you're a scalper you may start with the 5 minute chart for your levels and then switch to the 1 minute or even tick charts to execute your trades.

It is good to zoom out to a longer time frame in this way in order to get a clearer picture of the action. So for day traders, it will be much easier to come up with a handful of solid levels on the 30 to 60 minute chart. Staying on the 1 minute chart will tend to produce a plethora of levels, which could lead to overtrading.

Then, when you are in a trade, or putting on a trade, you want to see the price action at a much closer level (like a front row seat), so you move down to a shorter time frame again. Nowadays charting software makes it so easy to switch time frames that anyone can easily do this.

Prior swing highs

I find that in uptrends the market will pull back to prior swing highs for support. I generally find that the bigger reaction against the trend a swing high generates, the more likelihood it will act as future support. So a swing high that preceded a 5% pullback holds more weight in terms of future support probabilities than a swing high that preceded a 1% pullback. These levels are generally easy to spot on any time frame that is of interest to you. Figure 14 shows a daily chart of the S&P 100 index where a prior swing high acts as a support level.

Figure 14: Prior swing high as support level

Prior swing lows

In downtrends, I observe that prior swing lows can become resistance on retracement rallies. The same rules apply as with swing highs. The bigger the counter-trend move off the swing low, the better chance of it becoming a good level of resistance. Figure 15 shows an example in the Amazon daily chart.

Figure 15: Prior swing low as resistance

Pivots

Often key swing highs and lows can form pivot points that many professionals use to *fade* or counter the breakout. As the market auctions above a key swing high in search for buyers or below a key swing low in search for sellers, if there happens to be no interest generated the reversal can be quite swift. This is another reason why using prior swing highs and lows as support and resistance can be helpful in your trading. Figure 16 is an example of swing low pivots in a daily chart of the Dow Jones Industrial Index.

It's also important to note that the overnight highs and lows often come into play as potential pivots during the regular trading session.

The tendency of these pivots to occur at key swing highs and lows illustrates why I am not an advocate of placing stops directly above or below these levels, as these stops can become bull's eye targets for professionals.

Figure 16: Swing low pivots

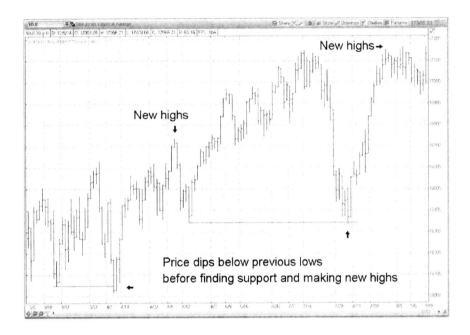

Open price gaps

The term *open price gaps* is used to describe closing prices that fail to get tested or filled during the next trading session. So if the S&P 500 closed at 1975 on a given day, 1975 would become the target for the gap to fill for the next day's trading. For example, the market might open higher the next day at 1980, which is a gap up, or it might open lower at 1970, which is a gap down. At some point in the trading day, gaps generally get filled, which means the 1975 settlement price in this example would be tested.

However sometimes, such as after a trend day, the previous settlement price fails to get tested and the market continues in the opening trend all day long, leaving behind an open gap. Oftentimes those open gaps eventually become a target when the current trend begins to get exhausted. These can be defined as potential future support or resistance, or at the very least a target for a trade. An example of this is shown in Figure 17 of the Russell 2000 ETF (IWM) daily.

Figure 17: An open price is later tested and filled

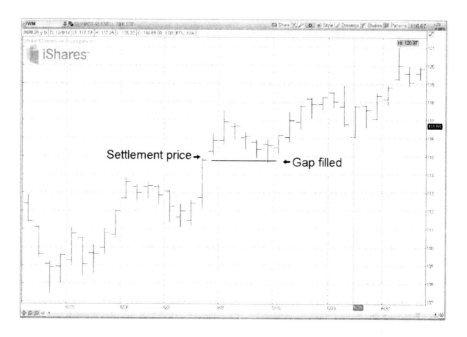

* * *

The combination of these easily defined support and resistance levels should help improve your odds when taken in context with the other elements discussed above, such as day type, gap type, open type, ATR, etc.

INSIDE DAYS

I want to take a moment to discuss the concept of inside days and why they are important. An inside day occurs when the current day's range from high to low is completely inside the previous day's range. I've added an example in Figure 18 to illustrate this point. Inside days typically occur on holidays or the day before a big economic data point, like the unemployment rate and non-farm payroll jobs numbers, or before an FOMC statement and monetary policy announcement. (You can find out exactly when these economic numbers are going to be released by looking at any one of the numerous economic calendars that are available online.)

Figure 18: Inside day

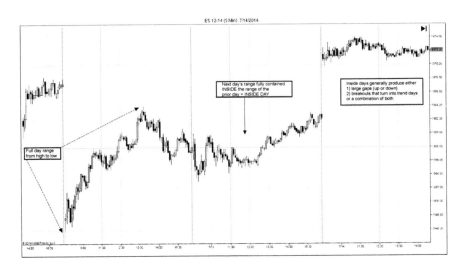

No matter what the external circumstances that caused it to occur, an inside day implies that buyers and sellers have temporarily agreed on a fair price and so there is no need for price discovery higher or lower until some new piece of information is released. So in the meantime, energy and volume levels build up inside this temporary fair value agreement. It is comparable to a can of fizzy drink that has been shaken up for a while. What happens when you finally open that soda can? An explosion, right?

That is generally what you get once this range is broken. It typically results in either a larger than usual gap up or down to start the day, or a breakout during the day session that turns into a trend day.

You should always be aware of inside days. They don't change any of the guidance in this playbook in terms of what to look for and trade off of, but they can change your expectations. There is a further example of an inside day and how it changes expectations in Figure 20, later in the book.

MARKET ENTRY

Another important concept to discuss is entries, or placing buy/sell orders to enter the market. There are two ways to do this. You can locate your price levels where you want to get long or short, put your orders in and let the market fill your order when those price levels trade. At that point there are only two possible outcomes: either your target will get hit or your stop will get hit. The benefit of this approach is that you are almost guaranteed to get the price you want, i.e. your ideal entry. The downside is that you are taking the risk of being run over – the trade turns against you and your stop is hit very quickly – if the volatility happens to pick up and you're on the wrong side of the trade.

The second way to enter the market is to watch the price action when it gets to important pivot levels, looking for confirmation of your analysis before you enter the trade. For example, let's say you have defined a resistance level on your price chart and a short trade fits your plans according to today's expectations based on the playbook.

Here you would watch the price action as it trades near the resistance level you have defined. What do you see? Do you see price action start to slow as it nears resistance? Are the rallies into resistance getting smaller and smaller in size and scope? If so, then placing your short trade becomes an opportunity. If not, and price rallies straight through your defined resistance level with little interruption, then you have got an answer without losing any money in the process.

The cons to this approach are you may find yourself taking drawdowns as the market retests support. You may then go on to beat yourself up, thinking that if you only waited for the perfect price level to enter, the trade would have worked out better. Another problem is that you will need a good deal of trading experience before being able to successfully pull this off – it is more of an art than a science.

In reality there is no perfect entry and exit and, personally, I've found the *wait and see* approach to be far superior in the long run, if it is taken into context of the big picture of the playbook. This approach generally takes some time to get used to. However, a thorough understanding of this playbook and what to look for in the market each day will shorten your learning curve dramatically.

TRADING DAY SITUATIONS

Now that we have an understanding of the different **day types**, **gap types** and **open types**, we can put all of this together so that we are prepared for whatever the market throws our way.

Every trading day will have one **day type**, one **gap type** and one **open type**. When these features are combined it gives a clear picture of the potential for either trend continuation or trend reversal. It also gives an idea of what days it may be acceptable to fade the market, like on rotational days looking for gap fills, and what days it may be best to trade with the trend and not attempt to fade at all.

An example of using the three pieces of information together is as follows:

- Previous day type: Up day

- Gap type: Up

- Open type: In range/above previous day's open

I will now work through a list of probabilities for each of the ten different market day scenarios. I will also gauge the conviction level of the short-term trend in each scenario. You will see that all possible situations are covered within the ten day setups. When you know which of the ten setups reflects the current market session, this enables you to make conclusions about the price action for that day.

After that, we will look at a recent example of each of the ten different scenarios using a 15 minute price chart of the E-mini S&P 500 futures contracts. We will go through the price action and see how each day could have been traded according to the playbook.

There is a summary of the ten day setups in the following table.

Note: Gap fill statistics for each setup are taken from the MastertheGap.com.

Ten day setups

Day setup	Previous day type	Gap type	Open type	Gap fill probability (%)
1	Up	Up	Above range	65
2	Up	Up	Inside range/above open (previous day)	85
3	Up	Down	Inside range/above open (previous day)	74
4	Up	Down	Inside range/below open (previous day)	65
5	Up	Down	Below range	48
6	Down	Up	Above range	54
7	Down	Up	Inside range/above open (previous day)	61
8	Down	Up	Inside range/below open (previous day)	74
9	Down	Down	Inside range/below open (previous day)	83
10	Down	Down	Below range	64

Day setup 1

Characteristics

- Previous day type: Up day
- Gap type: Up
- Open type: Above range

Rules

1. High odds of trend continuation, with a 65% chance of a gap fill or at least a test of the previous day's high at some point before the close.

2. Shorts for the gap fill should be light and should use the overnight high as the pivot. Taking out the overnight high – especially in the first 30 minutes – usually takes the gap fill trade off the table, so be cautious.

3. In the setup 1 scenario, the current day's open price becomes crucial; any attempted shorts should be light. If the buyers continue to defend the opening swing levels, shorts will likely fail. However, if sellers can take price below that opening swing this leaves the door open for the possibility of a test of the previous day's high and even the gap fill.

4. Longs near the high of the previous day and the gap fill or midpoint of the previous day (whichever is closest) are the ideal trade setup in this scenario. Longs should target the current day's open price, the overnight high and then the next resistance level above, or a full test of the Average True Range.

5. However, in certain cases where the market opens well above the previous day's range – which I denote by the market opening up by an amount roughly equivalent to the current ATR – a long setup near range or gap fill is likely off the table. In this case, initiating longs near the current day's opening swing is acceptable. One should generally wait the first 30 minutes, especially if a big economic report is due, before initiating longs there. The main point is to use the open swing as a stop out point or a line in the sand if the price drops below this level, especially on an unusually large gap up. By this I mean, if price fails to hold it's open price and it starts trading below, long trades should be abandoned because this open price may very well then become resistance for a rotation back into the previous day's high and possible gap fill/midpoint test of the prior day. The open price is a key level in a large gap up – it can be a difficult situation, but it generally pays to trade on the right side of that level (long above, short below).

Analysis

Figure 19 shows an example of this scenario. We had an up day for the previous day and a gap up above the prior day's range today. The previous day was an **inside day**, which means that the entire day's range from high to low occurred inside the range of the day before it. A gap above or below an inside day's range is generally not a move that you want to fade. A lot of energy and volume has built up in a small range, so the breakout generally becomes a trend.

Figure 19: Day setup 1

The larger than usual gap up after an inside day we can see in this instance would generally lower our expectations for a gap fill. Whereas if the previous day hadn't been part of an inside day, the gap fill or at the very least a test of the previous day's high would be a more realistic expectation.

This day turned out to be tricky as the gap higher resulted in an open well above the previous day's range, and made for a less than ideal risk-to-reward trade on the long side. In this scenario we have a previous day's range of about 10 points, but a gap up of about 10 points above the previous day's high. Here our first target for a long trade could be the overnight high, however the overnight high is only about a point and a half above the open price. So with a 2 point stop, this wouldn't even equate to a 1-to-1 risk-to-reward trade.

Secondly, as stated in the last bullet point of the rules for this type of day, on an unusually large gap up, waiting the first 30 minutes or so is usually prudent. In this chart example we see that the price opens, rallies to the overnight high, then fails at that level and price returns back and trades below the open price. This is a signal that there may not be any clear direction for the day and it is therefore best to trade smaller. Again, staying on the right side of the open price will be the best bet throughout.

It also needs to be considered that trend days have a tendency to occur when the open is against the prevailing short-term trend. For instance, a large gap up above the previous day's range has a greater chance to become an up trend day when the previous day was a down day. And vice versa, a large gap down below the previous day's range has a greater chance of becoming a trend day when the previous day was an up day.

My personal explanation for this phenomena comes from looking at the percentages for gap fills for each day type and how they decrease when the open is above the previous day's range for a down day and vice versa. My hunch is that longer-term traders get trapped on the trend reversal and have to unload their positions, thus increasing the velocity of the current day's open trend, adding fuel to the fire.

Even in this difficult scenario the playbook still worked effectively, as shorts near the overnight high showed some progress but could not push below the opening swing. This lack of follow through, along with the small break above the overnight high in the first 30 minutes, was a clear indication that shorts were probably not going to work today. At this point, only a break below today's opening swing would tempt me to get short.

Throughout the day, the market tested that opening swing level on three separate occasions after the initial 30 minutes of trading. The longs did show some success but unfortunately weren't able to make any substantial progress. Overall, this was a tough day for trading, as the total range for the entire day only equalled 5 points. I used this day as an example to show that even in these tough circumstances the playbook did a good job of informing you what to look out for.

Day setup 2

Characteristics

- Previous day type: Up day
- Gap type: Up
- Open type: Inside range/above open (previous day)

Rules

1. Moderately bullish setup that lacks the conviction of the **above range** open type. There is an 85% chance of gap fill at some time in the trading session. Trend continuation up is the higher probability scenario (especially with an open above the previous day's midpoint).

2. Shorting in anticipation of the gap fill should be the only counter trend trade to consider (if the risk-to-reward is favourable) and shorts should be light.

3. Use the previous day's session high and the overnight high as pivots for any attempt to short into the gap fill. A break above the higher of these two pivots (especially if it occurs in the first 30 minutes of trading), is a clear signal shorting is the wrong side to be on today.

4. Your ideal trade setups in this scenario will be longs near the gap fill and the midpoint of the previous day's session. If we happen to open below the midpoint of the previous day's session you can use the previous day's open price as a pivot for longs.

5. The target for longs becomes the current day's open price, the overnight high and the previous day's high.

6. A failure to hold above the previous day's open price or the overnight low (whichever comes in the lowest) is a clear warning sign of a short-term trend change. Longs should be exited on such a break down.

Analysis

Figure 20: Day setup 2

The example in Figure 20 depicts this scenario. The previous day ended as an up day and the current day's setup features a gap up above the midpoint and open, and inside the previous day's range.

Before we go any further, we have to note that this current day was an FOMC statement release day. Generally on these days, it is not a great idea to overtrade, or trade with a large position size, as whipsaw price movements are notorious. Even so, this example shows that no matter what is going on around you, more often than not the playbook will help to steer you in the right direction and keep your focus on the right trading setups.

The price opened right at the gap fill, so a short into the gap fill wouldn't have made a lot of sense from a risk-to-reward standpoint. We also had an overnight high pivot and the previous day's high in very close proximity to that same gap fill, so the long trade wasn't too attractive either (even though it would have worked).

However, the fact that those pivot levels above were taken out in the first 30 minutes of trading was a clear indication that the bullish bias was brewing under the surface. The market price eventually failed at the overnight high and previous day's high resistance, but only fell back into the midpoint of the previous day's trading. It happened very fast as the FOMC announcement was being released. The announcement is a time when you generally do not want to have open positions, but if you had the stomach for it, it turned out quite nicely as bulls took over from there and never looked back.

Day setup 3

Characteristics

- Previous day type: Up day
- Gap type: Down
- Open type: Inside range/above open (previous day)

Rules

1. There is a lack of conviction by both buyers and sellers. Trade lightly on both sides. The previous day's midpoint becomes crucial. An open below the midpoint usually gives the edge to sellers, whereas with an open above the midpoint the gap fill becomes a higher probability play (74%) and gives the slight edge to buyers.

2. On an open below the previous day's midpoint, initiate longs (they should be light) near the previous day's low and overnight pivots. Target that midpoint first and foremost. The gap fill is only possible on a breakthrough of that midpoint resistance, so be aware.

3. On an open above the previous day's midpoint, initiate longs near that midpoint or overnight low (whichever is closest) in anticipation of the gap fill and, in this case, the previous day's high and overnight high becomes a potential upside target as well.

4. On an open below the previous day's midpoint, shorts near that midpoint and the gap fill become the ideal setup. Targets become the overnight low and the low of the previous day's session.

5. Oftentimes the lack of conviction that characterises this type of day can lead to choppy price action and can also result in an inside day (where high and low of range are inside the previous day's range). This may be because of a Fed statement, important macroeconomic event or data point, etc. The market is saying it needs new information. This is a day type you generally don't want to overtrade in.

6. Judge the volume coming in during the overnight session, if it's well below average it may be best to stand aside for the day.

Analysis

Figure 21 is an example of this scenario, so let's walk through this day, step-by-step. As you can see, price opened above the previous day's open, but well below the midpoint. On this day, longs near the previous day's low made sense from a risk-to-reward standpoint; targeting the midpoint, first and foremost. However, shorts near the midpoint and gap fill are the ideal trade setup. So you had a choice to take the long trade, preferably with a small size, or wait for the midpoint test.

In this example, the risk-to-reward for the long side was good enough to take the shot. It worked well, as the previous day's low and overnight low provided the support necessary for the next rotation into the midpoint.

The next trade setup is the ideal setup given this day scenario and it worked perfectly. The sellers stepped up at that midpoint resistance area and took price down to a new range extension low, into a previously unfilled gap from two days ago.

Figure 21: Day setup 3

The setup was short at the midpoint. The first target is the previous day's low and the next target becomes the closest support level below according to the Average True Range, which in this example happens to be that unfilled gap. Both targets were achieved and the day turned out to be a success no matter what direction you decided to go in.

Day setup 4

Characteristics

- Previous day type: Up day
- Gap type: Down
- Open type: Inside range/below open (previous day)

Rules

1. This is a bearish warning sign of high probability weakness (at least off the open), especially when the open is below the midpoint of the prior day.

2. There is a 65% chance of a gap fill, but odds become worse on an open below the previous day's midpoint. At that point, it basically becomes a 50-50 toss-up.

3. Longs should be light, but can be initiated in a situation where the prior day's low or overnight low holds as support (whichever is lower). Longs should target the midpoint of the prior day (on an open below) or the gap fill (on an open above the prior day's midpoint). It's best to take profits on longs sooner rather than later with this day type.

4. Shorts are recommended as the trade that is more likely to be profitable in this day type scenario. Entry points near the gap fill or midpoint of the prior day are the most ideal. Targets for shorts would then be the prior day's low, the overnight low, and then the next identifiable support level below that coincides with the current Average True Range (ATR).

5. Oftentimes, this day type scenario can be the beginning of a short-term trend change, especially if there is follow through during the pit session, meaning if price continues to fall below the current day's open price. In this case, sellers would be following through on the bearish open type (especially on an open below the midpoint of the prior day). It becomes like a snowball, gaining momentum as it continues rolling downhill.

Analysis

Figure 22: Day setup 4

The 15 minute chart of the ES in Figure 22 shows an example of this day type. The previous day did finish as an up day per the criteria and closed higher than where it opened. The next day began with a gap down, in the range of the prior day but below both the midpoint and the prior day's open price. As noted in the bullet point rules above, this scenario paints a bearish picture, at least for the beginning of the trading session.

The ES opens right near the overnight low, as highlighted on the chart. There were two possible setups here: long near the overnight low targeting the midpoint of the prior session, or wait and see if there is a chance to get short near that midpoint level for the probability of a bearish continuation.

In this case, the long didn't make a whole lot of sense from a risk-to-reward standpoint (even though it would have been successful for targeting the midpoint of the prior day), as the potential entry was less than two points away from the target.

In this case, the probabilities (given this day type scenario) and risk-to-reward both favoured the short side. So it's no coincidence that this is indeed what worked. As the ES tested it's midpoint of the prior day, it was met with aggressive sellers looking to unload their contracts. The ES then proceeded to push lower, back below the prior day's low and overnight low. Around midday, the ES tried once again to rally, but was met with resistance at the prior day's low and then continued to move even further down to new intraday lows into the close.

Being aware of what day type was underway and what to expect in terms of probabilities would have suggested cutting counter-trend trades early and riding the momentum of the trades that were aligned with the trend probabilities.

Another warning sign was the break of the overnight low in the first 30 minutes. I have mentioned before that a break of an overnight pivot in the first 30 minutes is often a clear warning sign of a daily trend brewing.

I find this especially true when the market opens near the extreme of the overnight range and still takes out the pivot in the first 30 minutes. This example in Figure 22 did just that and that warning sign came to pass. As always, follow the guide for each day type scenario and pay attention to the warning signs and you will succeed.

Day setup 5

- Previous day type: Up day
- Gap type: Down
- Open type: Below range

Rules

1. Perception of value has shifted significantly overnight, usually due to a macroeconomic event. Short-term buyers will be underwater and are more likely to exit sooner rather than later. This has strong bearish implications, but can be tricky. If the open is significantly lower, the market may be too overextended to find a good risk-to-reward short entry point.

2. In the event of a significant gap down (the equivalent and opposite to the significant gap up described in the rules for day setup 1), longs should only be considered near the overnight low pivot and they should be light. Proceed with caution. Longs should target the low of the previous day's session and midpoint only.

3. A break below the overnight low in the first 30 minutes of trading (no matter how large the gap down), is a clear warning to exit any attempt to fade. In this situation trend day down probabilities become significantly higher.

4. This scenario has the lowest odds of producing a gap fill (48%).

5. Shorts near the previous day's low and midpoint are the ideal trade setups in this scenario.

6. This day type, unless reversed by the close, generally kick-starts a short-term trend reversal. This in turn may end up reversing the intermediate and long-term trend as well.

Analysis

Figure 23 shows an example of this scenario and how it played out. As you can see, the market opened well below the previous day's range. Being too overextended to make for a good momentum trade on a risk-to-reward basis, you had the choice of waiting for the retracement or taking a stab at the long side near the overnight low pivot.

In this case, the market held the overnight low during the first 30 minutes and it made for a good long setup into the low of the previous day's range. (Although this worked out well, long trades in general are to be small and treated with caution given this scenario.)

In fact the long setup actually continued to work right into the midpoint of the previous day's range (which should be considered the max upside target for longs in this scenario). Shorts at the previous day's low and midpoint worked as well, for those that waited.

Figure 23: Day setup 5

However, the short setups didn't produce the type of gains that the long side brought on this day. This can happen when the gap down is extreme in nature. Regardless, even in a difficult day type, solid trading opportunities on both the long and the short side were identified and they proved successful.

Day setup 6

Characteristics

- Previous day type: Down day
- Gap type: Up
- Open type: Above range

Rules

1. Some kind of macro event overnight has caused the perception of fair value to shift significantly.

2. Odds of a gap fill are 54%.

3. On a gap up significantly above the previous day's range (5 ES points or more), this will shift the odds to heavily favour a trend day up. Trapped shorts from the prior day will be getting squeezed and looking to exit at any price, resulting in higher prices.

4. Shorts targeting the prior day's high should only be taken near the overnight high pivot, and longs should be light.

5. Pay close attention to the current day's open. If the market spends the majority of the time below the open price this leaves the door open for a midpoint or gap fill opportunity.

6. If the market opens well above range, longs near the previous day's high are an ideal entry. The target is the current day's open, the overnight high and then the next resistance level above.

7. If the market opens just slightly above the previous day's high, then the risk-to-reward trade near that high is usually not ideal for an entry. In this case, it's best to wait for a long setup near the midpoint of the prior day and, of course, the gap fill.

8. Oftentimes, this day scenario results in a reversal of the short-term trend.

Analysis

Figure 24: Day setup 6

Figure 24 shows this day scenario. The previous day ended down and the current day begins with a gap up above range. This particular gap up was only 1 tick or a quarter of a point above range, so this was really close on the line.

In this case, the long at the high of the previous day's range didn't make a lot of sense from a risk-to-reward standpoint. The only opportunities would be to take small shorts near the overnight high or wait for prices near the gap fill or midpoint of the previous day's range.

The short setup occurred in the first 15 minutes of the day. Some people have rules against trading this early because of the potential for market orders and such. Personally, I find the first 30 to 60 minutes of the day the time where the best opportunities lie. My belief is to take shorts if this fits your plan and carries a healthy risk-to-reward setup. I may wait the first couple of minutes just to let things settle and the opening swing develop, but that is about it.

The only clear rule I have is to not place new orders right before a macro data point in the morning or an FOMC announcement in the afternoon.

In this case the short ended up working reasonably well. The market price broke below the current day's open and spent the majority of the first 30 minutes below it (which signals more potential downside). It resulted in further downside rotation near the gap fill and midpoint, which were just a couple of ticks apart. Unfortunately, the gap fill missed by a few ticks, but we know there is only a 54% chance of the gap fill given this day scenario (the second lowest odds of gap fill of the ten day scenarios). So it's prudent to anticipate such price action in advance.

The market price then found support and rotated back to the current day's open price (which is the first target), by the close.

Day setup 7

Characteristics

- Previous day type: Down day
- Gap type: Up
- Open type: Inside range/above open (previous day)

Rules

1. There are bullish implications for the day, especially if the open is above the previous day's midpoint. The gap has a 61% chance of being filled at some point before the close.

2. On an open above the previous day's midpoint look for long setups near the midpoint (since gap fill odds are on the low side) and at the gap fill, if the gap is filled.

3. On an open below the midpoint of the previous day, it's better to wait for the gap to fill before getting long. The overnight low and/or the previous day's open price is the key (whichever happens to be the lower price). Any break below those pivots, especially in the first 30 minutes, is a sign to abandon long trades.

4. Targets for long trades should be the midpoint of the previous day (if today opened below), the previous day's high and the overnight high, especially. Then look for a range extension to match the size of the previous day's range for a maximum upside target.

5. Shorts should be light and for the gap fill attempt only. On an open above the previous day's midpoint, look for a potential shorting opportunity near the overnight high or previous day's high, targeting the gap fill.

6. On an open below the previous day's midpoint, look for shorts near that midpoint level and overnight high, targeting the gap fill.

Analysis

An example of this day type scenario is depicted in Figure 25. The ES experienced a down day on the previous day that extended 7 points from high to low. The next day there was a gap up that was inside the previous day's range, but above the open and the midpoint of the prior day.

Our playbook suggests that in this type of scenario, a gap up above the prior day's midpoint has bullish implications overall, at least for the start of the trading day. However, the market presented a better short setup off the open, as the overnight high and the previous day's high were both in the vicinity.

Remember, shorts should be light and should target the midpoint of the previous day's range first and foremost. The odds of a gap fill are 61% given this day scenario, but that is one of the lowest odds of the ten different day scenario setups. Shorts should scale out and profits should be taken at the previous day's midpoint. After the numerous failed attempts to push lower, it was clearly better to close short positions and reverse long.

Figure 25: Day setup 7

The long setup at the midpoint was the ideal trade opportunity given the bullish implications of the day scenario. Not only did you have the midpoint support, but also the previous day's open price was only about 6 ticks below, adding some much needed confluence. After numerous failed attempts to push lower, the buyers stepped up the aggression and price pushed back up above the previous day's high and overnight high (which was first target for longs).

Then in this case when there doesn't happen to be any visible resistance above, we look at the most recent price history for clues, which happens to be the previous day's range from low to high. That range was about 7 points in length, so you would then add the 7 points to the low of the current day to come up with a logical target, which in this scenario and with recent regression of volatility, should probably be the maximum upside target.

This range target was achieved around the lunchtime hours and the market spent the rest of the day rotating inside the current day's range. Overall, there were some decent trading opportunities in this session, even with a lacklustre 7 point daily range.

Day setup 8

Characteristics

- Previous day type: Down day
- Gap type: Up
- Open type: Inside range/below open (previous day)

Rules

1. A low conviction open type for both buyers and sellers, it may lead to choppy price action. Be careful not to overtrade as there is potential for whipsaw price action.

2. The gap has a 74% chance of being filled. If the open is below the previous day's midpoint, shorts at resistance – the previous day's midpoint, the overnight high, or the previous day's open – are ideal. The target is a gap fill and then the overnight low (whichever comes first).

3. If the open is above the previous day's midpoint, longs are acceptable near the gap fill, midpoint and overnight low, targeting the overnight high and previous day's high.

4. A break above the previous day's high is a signal for a potential short-term trend reversal.

Analysis

Figure 26 shows an example of this scenario. The market opens up, above the midpoint of the previous day. Since the gap fill is a high probability given this setup, the short near the overnight high makes the most sense. In this case, it worked out rather well as price fell back down into a support zone that coincided with the gap fill, midpoint of the previous day and the overnight low.

The market then rotated back up to a new intraday high and proceeded to push even higher to take out the previous day's high as well. This was a day that offered a coupe of solid, high probability trading opportunities on both the long and the short side.

Figure 26: Day setup 8

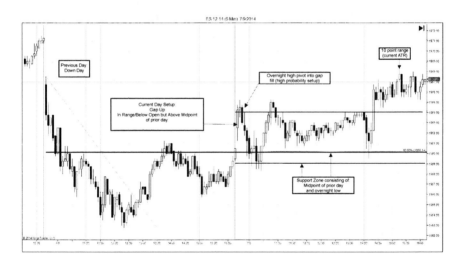

Day setup 9

Characteristics

- Previous day type: Down day
- Gap type: Down
- Open type: Inside range/below open (previous day)

Rules

1. There is an 83% chance of the gap filling before the close. Those odds go up if the open is above the previous day's midpoint.

2. On an open above the previous day's midpoint look for longs into the gap fill near the previous day's midpoint or overnight low. On an open below the midpoint, it's best to disregard long setups as this generally winds up being an ideal trend continuation setup.

3. Look for shorting opportunities near the gap fill and overnight high pivot, targeting the midpoint of the previous session (on an open above), the overnight low and the low of the previous day's session.

4. If the follow through on the downside fails to materialise (fails to break below the previous day's midpoint) by the afternoon session, especially on an open above that midpoint, that's a warning sign for shorts. In this situation, the odds favour short covering or buying into the close. This would likely take price above the high of the previous day's range, so look for that to be taken out to the upside.

Analysis

Figure 27 depicts a recent example of this scenario. The previous day was a down day and then the session opened with a gap down, inside yesterday's range and below its open. The open was above the midpoint of the prior day, as shown in the chart, which gives a chance that the long trade may work.

Unfortunately, the market price didn't trade down into the midpoint, which would have made for an ideal entry for the 83% chance of a gap fill. However, the counter trade setup did materialise, which was the short near the gap fill and overnight high pivots. This was a successful trade setup, as the market price rotated back down into the previous day's midpoint before finding support.

Figure 27: Day setup 9

At this point there were basically two options; if short from the gap and overnight high, at the very least profits should definitely be taken at the previous day's midpoint. The fact that the market price held that midpoint going into the afternoon session didn't bode well for further range extension to the downside. At this point it'd be highly advisable to take the money and run, even to the point of reversing and taking a stab at the long side (with a small position size).

If you missed or gave up on the short and were still waiting for more information before placing a trade, as the midpoint test evolved getting long near the midpoint made the most sense from a risk-to-reward standpoint. On this particular day it worked out very well. Not only did the market find support, it also reversed and made a new intraday high, even taking out the previous day's high briefly before the close.

This doesn't mean that this type of reversal should be expected every day. It's really all about aligning with the trend or the most probable outcomes and letting the market price do the work.

Day setup 10

Characteristics

- Previous day type: Down day
- Gap type: Down
- Type: Below range

Rules

1. A trend continuation setup with 64% chance of a gap fill.

2. Shorts near the midpoint of the previous day's session and the gap fill are the ideal trade setup. Shorting at the previous day's low should be small, however the probabilities and risk-to-reward are generally not as good. Targets for shorts should be the overnight low and the next support zone, lower.

3. If the gap down is well below the previous day's range, it's acceptable to use the overnight low pivot as a small long setup for the midpoint and gap fill possibility. If the overnight low is taken out, especially in the first 30 minutes, all longs should be abandoned.

4. For smaller gap downs it generally makes more sense to wait for shorting opportunities near the midpoint and gap fill.

5. If the gap down has come on a major macroeconomic event with heavy volume, any attempt to fade the gap should be eliminated.

6. Overall, short-term trend continuation is the probable outcome in this scenario.

Analysis

Figure 28 shows an example of this type of scenario. The market opened just below the range of the previous day, tested that range and failed in the first 15 minutes. At this point, any attempts at getting long should have been eliminated. The continuation of the short-term trend down was in full effect as price continued downward into a full test of the Average True Range and previously unfilled gap below, before finding support.

The trade setups were difficult on this day. Small shorts at the previous day's low would have worked out, and short positions could have been added to on the clear break below the overnight low. Small longs could have also been initiated at the unfilled gap support and a full test of the Average True Range, targeting the midpoint of the current day's session.

Figure 28: Day setup 10

So even though there weren't any ideal setups for full sized positions, having an understanding of the trend continuation probabilities in this scenario at the very least prevent you from getting run over. This is often just as good as a winning trade for the trader's mental and physical capital.

Dealing with neutral day types

Neutral day types are rare and so I do not give them much coverage in the playbook. If you do have a neutral day type, the best way to deal with it is to go ahead and trade in the direction of the prevailing short-term trend.

For example, if four of the last five trading days have finished as up days, I will usually stick with the prevailing theme and look for longs at nearby support, and vice versa in a short-term downtrend. Also be aware that a neutral day can be a sign of trend exhaustion, especially in an overbought or oversold market.

If you don't see much volume behind it, it is generally best to step aside for a while (the first hour of the day session) to let the initial balance develop and see if there are any clues for trend continuation versus trend reversal. You generally see these day types on a market holiday or the day before a big news event.

Dealing with neutral gap types

The same rules apply for neutral gap types as for neutral day types; these scenarios show an overall lack of conviction, at least off the opening swing. It is best to let the initial balance develop and look for clues of trend continuation versus trend reversal.

In these cases, overnight highs and lows are generally an important pivot point. Playing off the overnight range extremes in the direction of the short-term trend is often the best way to trade the beginning of the day. If the neutral gap comes on lower than usual overnight volume, maybe on a holiday, I would recommend staying out of the market that day altogether, as more than likely it will be a choppy session, unless some macroeconomic news event triggers.

Again, like neutral day types, neutral gaps are rare and thus I do not make much mention of them in the playbook. The general rule of thumb in these scenarios becomes: when in doubt *stick with the prevailing short-term trend*.

* * *

That concludes all the possible scenarios the market will throw at you within the day trading playbook. And it also gives you some likely outcomes given each opening scenario. Using the game plan described in this playbook – identifying support and resistance, understanding the Average True Range concept to give your expectations a foundation, and gaining an understanding of your personal risk profile and how to think in terms of risk-versus-reward – will put you on a firm foundation for trading success and shorten your learning curve.

Swing Trading
Playbook

INTRODUCTION

In this book you have already been introduced to a simple and effective system for day trading. Now we will take a look at a swing trading system. Encompassed within this is a general system for analysing the current market situation.

Swing trading is a technique employed by traders to capture bigger moves in the market over the short to medium term. Swing traders are somewhere in the middle between day traders, who look to enter and exit positions in the same day, and buy and hold investors, who aim to grow their investments over five to ten years, or even longer.

Some swing traders look to hold positions for one to four days at a time, and then there are others who, maybe due to constraints on the time they are able to devote to market analysis, look to hold positions for weeks or months at a time.

The method of swing trading presented in the playbook will work for you whether you are a shorter-term or longer-term swing trader. All that will really change is the price chart you are looking at. Short-term swing traders will generally look at daily and 60 minute price charts and longer-term swing traders will generally stick with weekly price charts.

As in the day trading section, we will look at each component individually, with examples. Then the section will finish by putting it all together with more examples of real swing trading examples, which I will walk through step-by-step.

Many of the following examples depict long setups and there are two reasons for this. The tremendous bull market experienced in the last five years leaves few recent examples for shorting opportunities. Also, over the long run the market generally favours the long side. This does not mean the playbook doesn't work for the short side – we will see enough short examples to debunk that idea.

One piece of advice I offer for newer traders is to begin by sticking to one side of the trade. In my opinion you should stick to the side of the prevailing macro trend until you have more trading experience.

In the following, I will present many examples of both index funds and individual stocks. I will also present examples from the present and historical price action, just to show that these methods are time tested and not a fad due to algorithm trading or an equivalent.

So let's begin.

IDENTIFY THE TREND

The first individual concept to discuss is the trend of the market. Every trader is told from day one, the trend is your friend. And with swing trading, one of the most important elements is defining that trend.

Sadly, many in the trading community have resorted to elaborate systems to define the trend. I've tried many of them myself, when I first started learning, however I found little benefit from overcomplicating things.

On the contrary, the things I will show you are simple to understand and implement, and they have stood the test of time. As we will see, these tools will work for individual stocks as well as the major averages (basically they work for anything with volume). So no matter what vehicle you trade, or what style you trade in, you will find something useful in this section.

Moving averages

In defining the trend, we can begin with a simple concept. Figure 29 is a daily chart of the S&P 500. One way to identify the trend is to simply look at the direction of the 50 and 200 day moving averages and trade in that general direction. In the example, we see both the 50 day and 200 day moving average clearly going in an upward direction. In this case it bodes well to stick with long setups. Simple as that.

Figure 29: Using moving averages to identify trend

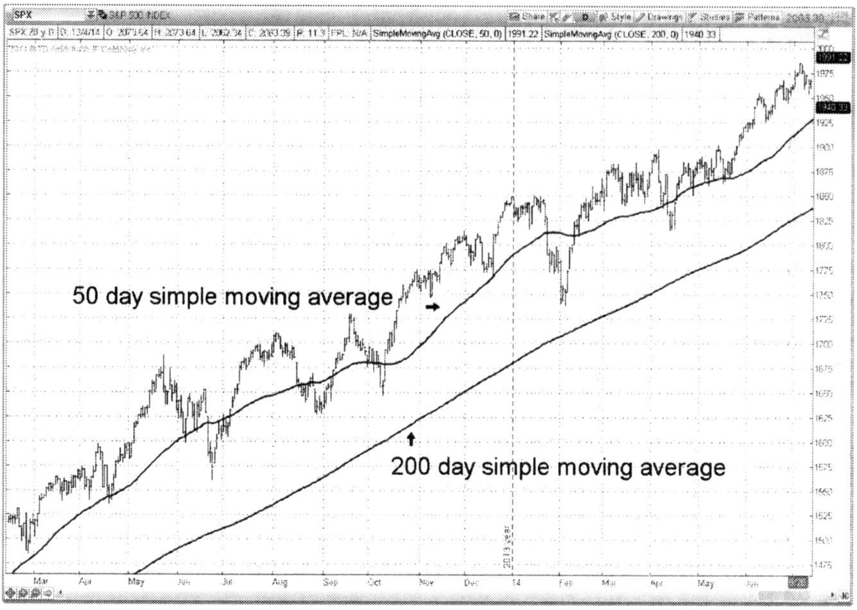

Let's now add a further element into the mix.

Closing above the previous bar

Using the same chart, let's say we call a buy signal on any daily price bar that closes above the previous bar after a multi-day decline. Over the past 12 months you would have received 12 separate buy signals. I have highlighted each of these signals in Figure 30 using an arrow. The numbered arrows represent successful signals/winning trades. Arrows with no numbers represent failed signals/losing trades.

I define a losing trade as a failure to make a new high and a reversal below the low that was left behind before the buy signal. I define a winning trade as a trade that made a new high without taking out the swing low left behind prior to the signal.

Figure 30: Buy signals on closing above the previous bar

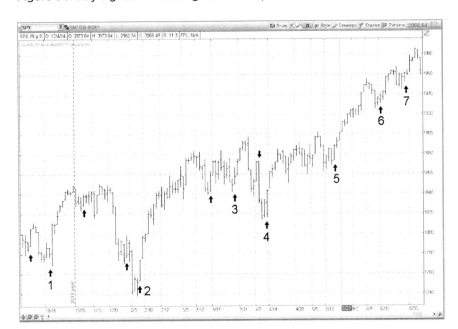

Using this criteria would have resulted in seven winning trades and five losing trades, or a 58.3% winning percentage. If you couple that with good money management skills, you've got a better trading system than most black boxes could ever offer.

We don't want to take every signal, so we can do even better by only taking the signals that correspond with one of the other tools which I will discuss next. Before we do, let's make sure we understand this concept and how to use it effectively.

Figure 31 shows a zoomed in version of the exact chart we just looked at in Figure 30. We can see one of the buy signals that worked. Now remember a buy signal is generated on a close above the previous day's high after a multi-day decline.

For the purposes of this example, let's assume this particular long setup had some added confluence that validated the signal and made it worth the risk. In this case you could buy just before the close, since it's obviously above the previous day's high, or wait and buy the next day's open price. You would then use a stop level just below the actual swing low left behind before the buy signal occurred.

Figure 31: Zoomed in portion of Figure 30

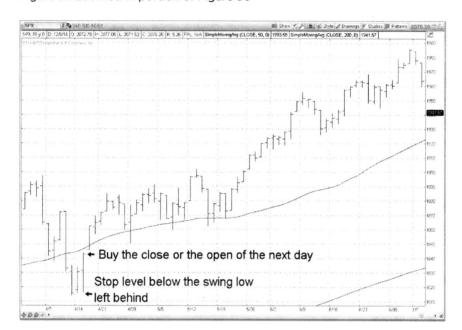

Again, this is just one piece of the puzzle, so at this point I won't go into upside targets and what exactly those added confluence indicators might be. For now, just get an understanding of each piece of the puzzle and we will put it all together later in the chapter.

SUPPLY AND DEMAND (MEASURED MOVES)

Next, I will talk about supply and demand. When you really think about it, every move in the market is based upon supply and demand. Contrary to popular belief, especially in the financial media, there are actually never more buyers than sellers, and on the flip side there are never more sellers than buyers. Every trade has one buyer and one seller, end of story. What really moves price is the aggressiveness of the buyer or the seller to get their own way.

In 2008 at the height of the financial crisis, it was a scary time for everyone. People feared the worst, they feared losing everything. In the height of the panic, many investors were running for their lives and were willing to sell at any price just to be out of the stock market and out of harm's way. This aggressiveness on the part of the sellers is what caused the prices of every risk asset to plummet. All of a sudden you had this massive supply shock. Market makers had to feverishly match all these sell orders with buyers. In order to do this effectively, they had to lower and lower prices to attract those buyers.

On the other side, we had the great dot.com bubble of 1999 and 2000. Computers and technology were advancing at a rapid pace and the internet made everything easier, including buying stocks. In turn, everyone wanted a piece of the action and frantically bought any technology company, especially new companies, many of which were not even making a profit. The strong demand from the public and institutions alike drove prices higher and higher.

The simple truth is that supply and demand affects every market, every asset class and every individual stock. As an investor, one must be aware of the fundamental aspects of the company and prospects for the future. But as a trader, the single most important piece of information you have is the supply and demand pattern of each market you are interested in. The best way to track these supply and demand patterns is simply by studying the price chart.

The simplicity of supply and demand is found by measuring the sizes of both the rallies and the declines by points. I call these **measured moves** and I will further elaborate on these concepts in the following examples.

Measured moves

The first example of supply – shown in Figure 32 – uses the popular momentum stock Tesla (symbol: TSLA). In the 12 months covered by the chart, Tesla has experienced two separate declines in stock price. The supply, or you could say oversupply, is measured by looking at the difference from the highest close to the lowest close of the most recent market movement. A measurement is also taken for the difference between the highest intraday high price and the lowest intraday low price.

The reason that this second measurement is taken is to ensure all bases are covered. In most cases, the high to low closing prices will equate to a lower overall point total than the intraday high to low and if this is the case then that is the measurement to use. However, we don't want to be waiting for a full measured move only to end up watching the swing trade opportunity pass us by, so if the measurement between the highest intraday high price to the lowest intraday low price is lower then we use that instead.

Figure 32: Tesla

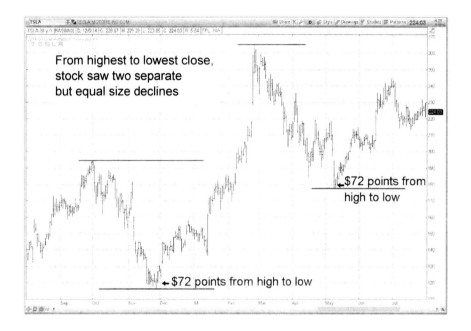

So in this particular example, the high to low closing prices in both of these price swings resulted in moves of exactly 72 points in length, while the intraday high to low price swing resulted in a move of 78 points. This is why it's always best to stay aware of both.

So around April to May in the chart many no doubt gave up on Tesla and left it for dead. In reality, all that had happened was a short-term supply imbalance that matched the size of the previous pullback, which resulted in an excellent swing trade long setup. Once Tesla's share price reached that retracement size, the stock found support and rallied some 36% off its low.

At that point it may very well have continued towards yet another 52 week high; that likely depends on the trend of the broader market. What we do know is that by paying attention to the recent supply pattern of this stock, we were able to uncover an optimum buy area when many were likely selling at the wrong time.

Let's put together the two topics we have learned so far. Let's say we take the buy signal (close above the previous day's high), once that full measured move retracement is in reach. In this way we filter out some of the signals and improve our analysis of the swing trade in a simple and effective way.

Measured move in reverse

Figure 33: Measuring potential rallies

We can also use the measured move concept in reverse to estimate the size of potential rallies and come up with a logical upside target. On the daily chart in Figure 33, we can see the iShares Russell 2000 ETF (IWM), which tracks the small cap Russell 2000 index.

The market was in a clearly defined uptrend. Once support was established, the first tool we can use as a measuring stick is the size of the previous advance, which was just over 11 points. We would then add that to the swing low that formed to arrive at a logical upside target. That target was achieved and the market actually found resistance at that projected measured move upside target as well, which leads me to my next point.

Figure 34: Two similar-sized drops in Vanguard REIT Index ETF

Figure 34 shows a weekly chart of the Vanguard REIT ETF (VNQ). In 2011, the REIT sector was hit badly (losing over 20% in a period of a few weeks), but recovered very well. Less than a year later this ETF had erased all of the losses of the prior year and continued its upward trajectory.

Then later in 2013, following a comment from the then Chairman of the Fed about a monetary policy change, the REIT sector once again experienced selling pressure. Once the short-term trend was clearly broken, we turn to the long-term chart to study the recent history.

Matching up the prior $17 point correction from 2012 to the new highs in 2013, we can see that the 2013 correction was almost equal to the previous correction ($16 as compared to $17). This drop of $16 took the price roughly to the level of the prior swing high before the last major sell-off and this level then came in as support. The combination of those two factors – the $16 drop and reaching the prior high level – was enough to stop the bleeding, as the price found support and then continued to move higher up to the end of the chart.

That is the theory of supply and demand, and how it can easily be applied to swing trading analysis of market direction and trend strength.

Measuring corrections by percentage

The other thing I wish to discuss in this section is measuring corrections by percentage. I have described measuring declines by points, which is always your starting point, but you should always be aware of recent declines by percentage as well.

This goes especially for stocks. Consider a high growth stock like Tesla. It could experience a 12 point drop when the stock price is $60, which is a 20% correction, but then if the stock price shoots up to over $200 a similar $12 point drop is now not much of an event. So it's good to be aware of both percentage and points measurements.

In this situation, if Tesla's stock price looked to be in full correction mode, you would want to see if there are any confluence areas around the $160 level – this would match the 20% decline seen when the stock was trading at the $60 level.

Figure 35: Daily chart of the S&P 500 from 2009

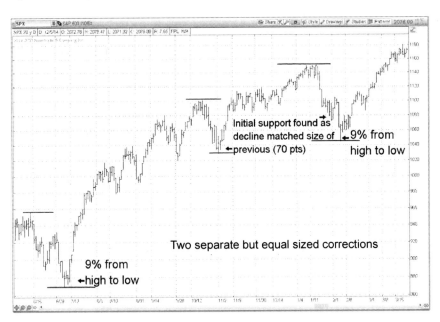

Figure 35 shows a daily chart of the S&P 500 going back to the beginning of the bull market in 2009. Midway into 2009, the broad market experienced a 9% correction before finding support and continuing higher.

The stock market continued its upward trajectory into the beginning of 2010, at which point the euro zone headlines really started to hit the wires and rattle markets. The S&P 500 first dropped 80 points, which matched the size of the most recent correction, briefly found support, but then turned south once again. However, once the market got into the 9% correction area, which matched the size (as a percentage) of the mid-2009 pullback, the market found the support to take prices higher.

The rule of thumb is look for the pullback to match the size (in points) of its previous correction on whatever time frame you are trading – daily, weekly, 60 minute, it doesn't matter. If that fails to hold, then look for the last correction size in terms of percentage. If the result projects support well below the initial entry then it is probably best to take the small loss and look for a better entry. If the projected support area is still within reach, it probably makes the most sense to stick with the current trade and targets.

Figure 36: Amazon chart from 2010

Our next example comes from Amazon (AMZN). Figure 36 is a monthly chart going back to the lows of 2010. Each of the three corrections in the stock price since 2010 have resulted in 30% pullbacks.

Let's take the most recent correction as an example. Once you see a reaction against the prevailing trend that is larger in size (points) than any of the previous reactions leading up to the most current high, you must assume that longer-term traders or investors (or maybe you use the term *smart money*) are involved. In that case, you must look at the macro picture and get an understanding of what has happened in the past to give you a higher probability chance of making a good decision for the future.

What you would do is then look at your longer time frame chart and now we see a 30% correction has been the typical pattern. You don't just mark off 30% from the high and then sit there with a limit buy order. Instead, you want to look for a support region somewhere in the vicinity of that 30% retracement area.

If you have a support zone in the area of a 28% correction then don't sit and hold out for the full 30% – because you may not get it. In this example, there was a prior swing high on the monthly chart, which is a great place for a potential support zone on a pullback. It did happen to be in the vicinity of the full 30% retracement and it worked very well. Following that, the stock moved up 20% and continued higher.

Like I mentioned in the day trading section, don't fixate on trying to buy the low tick and sell the high tick of every move; this is impossible. There are way too many moving pieces and emotions at work in the financial markets to be able to consistently achieve perfection. Instead, focus on what is possible and try to accomplish that as well as you possibly can. This example worked out about as well as anyone could possibly hope for, but that doesn't mean every setup is going to work as well.

Judging when a retracement is over

How do you know when the retracement or correction is over?

Well, the actual answer is, you don't. But one rule of thumb that I use is to measure the size of the biggest retracement rally inside the decline. If the buyers can push price off the swing low that gets left behind, farther in size (points) than any of the previous retracements, the chances are good that the correction is over (especially if the rally is coming off a confluence area like the one in the Amazon example above).

Let's take a moment to discuss this using the same company, Amazon, on the daily chart in Figure 37. Let's focus on the retracement rallies. We are going to use the closing prices only. Remember, it's important to pay attention to both closing prices and intraday highs and lows.

Figure 37: Amazon daily chart

During Amazon's retracement rally, after the initial wave of selling took prices to lower lows, buyers were able to push the stock price up $32 points off the lows before the next wave of selling began. Next on the chart, you can see one failed attempt at a rally, only taking prices up a little over $20 points on a closing basis before falling again.

Finally, after reaching a support zone with a prior swing high and a full 30% correction for the third time in recent history, Amazon's share price was able to push higher than the previous two attempts at a rally and continued higher to the end of the chart.

Again, I will expound on all of this in the swing trading examples later in the section. For now just make sure you grasp each of these concepts.

BOX THEORY

There is an old book called *How I Made $2,000,000 In The Stock Market*, which tells the story of a man named Nicolas Darvas. During the 1950s and 1960s, he used a method called the **box theory** to achieve large profits in the stock market.

The book goes into detail about his story and his emotions during his journey to riches. While it doesn't talk about his methods in any detail, there are some charts that give the general idea. After attempting to replicate the method in real time, I will describe the best way I have found to use it.

Replicating the box method

Figure 38: Using box theory on the iShares S&P 600 SmallCap Index Fund

For the example in Figure 38, I have used a daily chart of the iShares S&P 600 SmallCap Index Fund. The first thing you have to do is locate a trading range. Generally, what you want to look for is an area where there has been up and down price action inside of a range, resulting in at least two touches of either support or resistance. The price ranges doesn't have to be exact, as long as the highs and lows are assembled in the vicinity of the others inside of the range.

Having located the trading range, the next step is to identify the lowest low and the highest high point (on both an intraday and closing basis) and then subtract the low from the high and the resulting number is the total range size. You then add the length of that prior range to the high of the range to come up with a logical estimate for an upside target.

Generally there won't be much of a difference between the intraday and closing figures, unless there is an unusually volatile event such as an FOMC statement announcement or a flash crash. The main point is to get an estimation and then look for confluence support/resistance level that would be in that general vicinity.

For this example, the trading range was about 5.50 points from low to high. We then add the 5.50 points to the high at $87.64 to come up with an estimated upside target of $93.14. The actual swing high came in at $93.27, achieving our upside target before a correction that actually saw price fall back into support, which came in right at the high of the previous trading range that price had broken out from.

I talked about how previous swing highs can become support on corrections during the support and resistance chapter of the day trading section. This is yet another example of how these methods can be universally applied to any time frame or investment vehicle.

Another example of the box theory method is shown in Figure 39. Here we have a daily chart for Cognizant Technology Solutions (CTSH). We have almost a two-year trading range with about $13 points from high to low.

Finally, late in 2013 there was breakout above this trading range. At this point we would then simply add the size of the trading range to the high that was left behind to come up with a logical projection for a target.

In this case, it equated to roughly $53.50. The stock price didn't waste much time in getting there. Not only did the price target for longs work, the projected target also acted as resistance and the stock actually pulled back more than 10% after hitting the target.

Figure 39: Box theory with Cognizant Technology Solutions

Although the box theory was originally meant for the buy side only and the two examples just shown feature breakouts to the long side, the same general principles can be reversed to apply to stocks and indices in obvious downtrends.

Let's take a look at an example.

Using box theory in a downtrend

Figure 40 shows a daily price chart for the stock CF Industries (CF). After the stock made a new high it began to trade range bound, with multiple touches of the low of the range and two distinct tests of the high of the range. The sum total of the entire range from high to low equated to 17 points in length.

When the stock eventually broke the trading range to the downside, a downside target can be projected by using the length of the prior range and subtracting that from the low of the now broken trading range.

Figure 40: Applying box theory in a downtrend on CF Industries

That calculation gives a projection of $233 for a price target below and that is exactly how it all played out. Only two days after the break down the stock price was testing that $233 level and it became an excellent support level (as it not only worked on the first test, but three separate times it was tested and was successful support).

The price subsequently broke back to the upside and inside the previous trading range.

MEASURING HIGHER HIGHS/LOWER LOWS

In this section, I want to talk about another form of measuring the level of supply and demand in the markets by noting the higher highs or lower lows that are forming. I will show how to measure how far the higher highs go above the previous high in an uptrend and how far the lower lows go below the previous low in a downtrend.

What we want to accomplish in this is twofold. Number one, we want to see if there is a pattern developing. Does the market breach a previous high by a certain number of points each time? Number two, we want to see if there may be a weakening of the underlying trend that is noted by the market. Maybe price is not pushing above its previous high as far as it has in the recent past, or the lower lows are coming in closer and closer together, which would suggest the downtrend is weakening and sellers aren't able to push price as low as they once could. These are the sorts of things we are looking for.

Patterns developing with new highs or lows

Figure 41: New highs in the Dow Jones Industrial Average

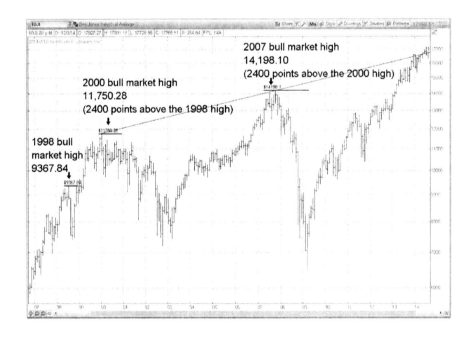

One of the most glaring examples of this pattern can be seen in the long-term chart of the Dow Jones Industrial Average, shown in Figure 41. The bull market high in the year 2000 came in 2400 points above the 1998 bull market high. Fast forward seven years and we see that the 2007 bull market topped out at exactly 2400 points above the bull market high of the year 2000. This preceded the biggest stock market decline since the early 1970s.

That same extension played out again as the DJIA moved 2400 points above its 2007 bull market high. The market then underwent a brief correction that took the major average down almost 10%.

It eventually recovered and was able to push higher and break the long-term pattern that had been in place for over 14 years. This is one of the reasons I continue to remain optimistic on stocks for the long run, even though it may be a volatile ride; I think that the probabilities suggest a continued upward trajectory.

Figure 42: A pattern in new highs in the S&P 500

On a more micro level, Figure 42 shows a daily chart of the S&P 500 index. Here we can see three separate occasions where there was a push 35 points higher than the previous high, before resistance was found and a pullback began.

Strength/weakness of the trend

As mentioned, this method can be used to gauge the strength or weakness of the prevailing trend, as we will see in the next example.

Figure 43: Measuring lower lows to spot the end of the trend

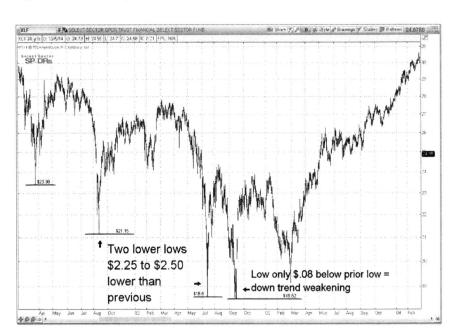

In Figure 43, we have a daily chart of the financial sector index exchange traded fund (XLF) during the final stages of the 2000 to 2002 bear market decline. The first lower low came in about $2.25 points below the previous low before a retracement rally occurred. The rally failed to take prices to new highs and then proceeded to continue its downward trajectory. Eventually prices were taken to another lower low, this time about $2.50 points below the prior low.

At this point, another retracement rally kicked off, which took price back up to about the midpoint of the last swing high to low, before resistance was found once again and the downtrend continued into yet another lower low.

On this third lower low something different happened. Instead of dropping another $2+ points below the low at $21.15, the resulting sell side activity was only able to take the price about $0.08 cents below the prior swing low before reversing higher. This was a clear indication of the potential of underlying strength to finally reverse prices and end this downtrend.

In the end that is what played out. Although there was another sharp drop in the market price, the resulting selling pressure failed to materialise into another lower low and in turn the baton was passed over to the buyers who took over and broke the downtrend. For a few years at least.

A-B-C CORRECTIONS

The next topic I want to cover is A-B-C corrections.

The term **A-B-C correction** will be familiar to many traders from Elliott Wave theory. I studied Elliott Wave for some time and, although it has merit, personally I thought it was too complicated and came with too much of a hindsight bias. What I mean by this is that it seemed to work better when looking backwards at completed price action rather than analysing current action. Also, it tends to be prone to subjective revisions. When I use the term A-B-C corrections and the general concept I apply it in a simpler and more straightforward method.

I find that oftentimes corrections inside of an uptrend play out in three waves (A-B-C). The first wave (A) is the initial supply shock that generally catches people off guard at first. It usually drops the stock or index further than a previous correction size experienced in the recent past. The second wave (B) becomes the retracement, usually back to the midpoint of the last swing high to the first wave down's low, or maybe to resistance at the low of the now broken trading range.

Whatever the case may be, the retracement ends up as a short setup for another wave down (C) to a new lower low. Usually this wave down mirrors the size of the initial wave down and often ends the correction after finding support at a previous swing high or other confluence area. I find it fascinating how well and how often this phenomenon plays out.

A-B-C waves in real-life charts

Let's look at an example of an A-B-C correction on a macro level. Figure 44 is a monthly chart for the stock Google (GOOGL) going back to the year 2007-2008. From late 2007 into early 2008, the initial wave resulted in the stock price dropping $170 points, taking out the prior low decisively. Then a relief rally ensued that took the price back to the midpoint of the initial selling shock.

Figure 44: A-B-C correction in Google

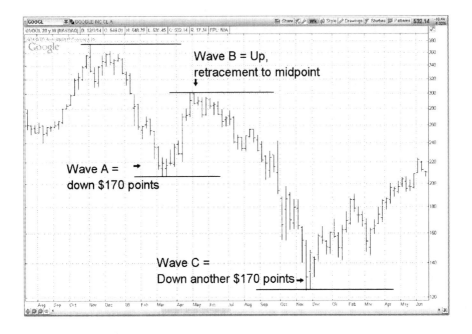

This proved to only be a retracement into the next short setup as sellers came back in fury to take prices down to new lows. The result was a third and final selling wave lower that took the price down roughly $170 as well, almost exactly matching the size of the initial selling wave. By 2009, the selling had dried up and Google's stock price continued to appreciate some 600% over the next five years.

Now let's take a look at an example on a more micro scale. The 60 minute chart of the S&P 500 in Figure 45 shows two pullbacks in the benchmark major average. They both show classic traits of the pattern with two separate selling waves down and a retracement rally in the middle. Each pulled back to a support level defined by a prior swing high.

Figure 45: Two A-B-C pullbacks in the S&P 500

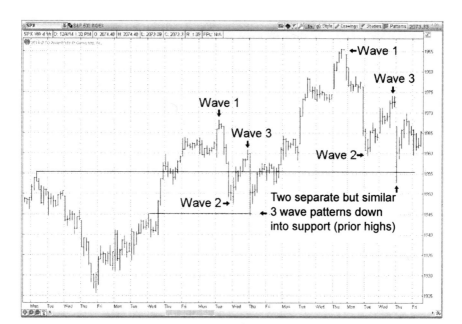

When should you expect an A-B-C correction as opposed to a typical one wave of selling into support?

My rule of thumb is, if the market experiences an initial supply shock that is greater in length than any of those in recent history, more often than not it then follows through with an A-B-C style correction with one more lower low before completion. If you get a correction that is in line with the corrections of the recent past, more often than not it becomes just a blip along the way and the trend will usually continue.

Also remember the same concepts that you are learning here for the long side will work in reverse on the short side when in a downtrend.

MARKET INDICATORS

There are countless market indicators available for you to choose from. Personally I have tried almost every single one of them and I have come to the conclusion that there are really only three indicators that you need:

1. New York Stock Exchange (NYSE) advance-decline line.

2. S&P 500 advance-decline line.

3. St. Louis Fed Financial Stress Index.

Advance-decline lines

An advance-decline line calculates every stock that advances (or closes positive) and every stock that declines (or closes negative) for each day, and it gives the total number for each day.

Generally I will focus mostly on the S&P 500 advance-decline line, but the NYSE indicator is a good barometer as well. It includes many more stocks, so it often can give a better picture of the broader market.

There are two ways to view each indicator. One is a daily count, which adds the advancers and subtracts the decliners to come up with a total number, which generally will either be positive if it's been a good day for the market or negative if it's been a bad day. The other way is a cumulative view of each day's total reading, which is the optimal way to analyse market movements. I'll discuss each of these methods in the following examples.

I recommend stockcharts.com as the best place to get your market indicators. You can get up to three years of data for free. If you want to go further back in time to do some back testing, you can do that for a reasonable monthly rate.

The ticker symbol to access these market internal indicators is $SPXADP for the S&P 500 advance-decline line and $NYAD for the NYSE. It defaults to the daily readings. To get the cumulative version, all you have to do is click the drop down arrow next to the 'type' category under the chart attributes section.

Daily readings

The first way to view this indicator is by using the daily readings. The purpose is to locate extreme readings, that if near support or resistance levels may end up being an ideal entry for a swing trading position.

Figure 46: Daily S&P 500 advance-decline line

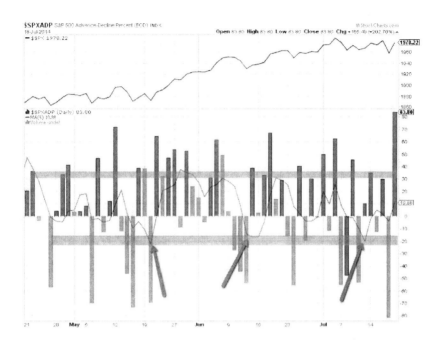

Figure 46 is an example using the S&P advance-decline line by percentages for each trading day. I have placed a five day moving average over the chart to smooth out the daily fluctuations. What you can see is that over the last few months when the moving average hits the -20% area, it's generally been a good time to be buying.

You can also look at the extreme readings, like the one on the far right of the chart that hit the -80% reading for the day. That meant that 80% of the stocks in the S&P 500 closed in negative territory that day. While you certainly don't want to be fading every extreme reading in either direction, it can be helpful to take the signals that also have confluence support or resistance areas and which are generally in line with the direction of the overall trend.

Cumulative readings

Now we turn our focus to the cumulative readings of these indicators. I view these as the rudders of the ship. It's extremely hard for the major averages to continually make new highs if the advance-decline line cannot make new highs alongside it, and vice versa.

Figure 47: Cumulative NYSE advance-decline line

In Figure 47, we see the cumulative reading on the NYSE advance-decline line with a chart of the S&P 500 index above it. You can see the strength in the advance-decline line during the year 2012 when the S&P 500 didn't make a whole lot of progress in comparison. However, this strength continued to follow through into 2013 when the major averages really started to take off to the upside, putting in an annual return for 2013 of over 30%.

That underlying strength continues to the end of the chart, which doesn't leave the market bears a whole lot to work with. These type of indicators help make it clear what the trend of the market is and reinforce what direction you should be trading in.

You can also add your standard 50 and 200 day moving average to these charts if that helps you to visually keep track of the prevailing trend.

Figure 48: Cumulative S&P 500 advance-decline line

Figure 48 shows the cumulative S&P 500 advance-decline line by percentages. As you can see on the chart, there wasn't as much upside momentum in 2012 as the NYSE displayed (which is one reason to watch both indexes). However, things really started to take off in 2013 and confirmed the corresponding upward momentum in overall stock prices.

Even though there were a number of legitimate reasons to get out or short the market during this time, one look at these internal readings would clearly show you that it was going to be a steep uphill battle and probably not something worth fighting against.

I find these indicators extremely valuable, because they help to eliminate biases that may occur in the individual for a variety of different technical and fundamental reasons.

These advance-decline indicators are mostly used to analyse the market and the strength underneath, but as we saw in the previous example, they can also be used to create a signal to enter or exit the market as well.

St. Louis Fed Financial Stress Index

Figure 49: St. Louis Fed Financial Stress Index

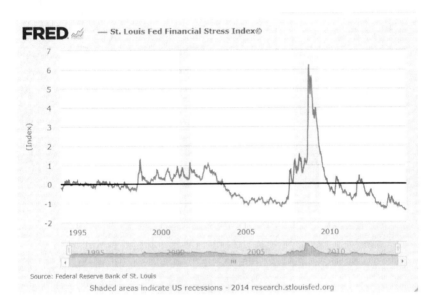

Another indicator I find extremely helpful is the St. Louis Fed Financial Stress Index. I am not an economist, so I use this index as my guide. I find it does a wonderful job of gauging the degree of financial stress in the markets, by focusing on a wide array of economic indicators from different interest rates to yield spreads, among others.

According to the website (research.stlouisfed.org/fred2/series/STLFSI), the average value of the index is designed to be zero. Readings below zero suggest below-average financial market stress, while values above zero suggest above-average financial market stress. These readings are released on a weekly basis.

I encourage you to visit the St. Louis Fed website to get the Financial Stress Index chart and weekly readings. You can also get more information on all of the different data series that the index uses to come up with its weekly readings.

Combining the cumulative advance and decline line and the St. Louis Fed Financial Stress Index, you have a solid foundation to form your market analysis and macro views. It is also useful to add the Volatility Index (VIX) into your analysis, which I will discuss next.

THE VOLATILITY INDEX (VIX)

I briefly discussed the Volatility Index (VIX) in the day trading section. We can also use the VIX as a barometer for expectations of future market movements and trading possibilities. The parameters that I find most helpful are as follows (I will discuss them in more detail below):

- **VIX readings below 20** = Day trading opportunities are limited; swing trading long setups are preferred.

- **VIX readings between 20 and 40** = Optimal area for day traders, as the added volatility makes for larger intraday ranges, but it is not so volatile that things are out of control. Swing trading setups for both long and short opportunities are acceptable.

- **VIX readings above 40** = Significant downside risk potential, swing trading opportunities on the short side only should be considered. Day trading opportunities are plentiful, but the increased volatility could make even this very risky. Proceed with caution.

I know some traders look at divergences in the VIX, so if the VIX is making a higher low while the S&P 500 is making a new high, they would then take this divergence as an ominous threat to the uptrend and assume a pullback is forthcoming.

Personally, I don't find this at all helpful; this is easily something that can make you overanalyse the situation and get you out of a position that is likely to continue working. There are just way too many moving parts in the calculation of the Volatility Index to infer any confirmation from its readings in terms of divergences.

Figure 50: VIX monthly closing price chart with best course of action for each zone

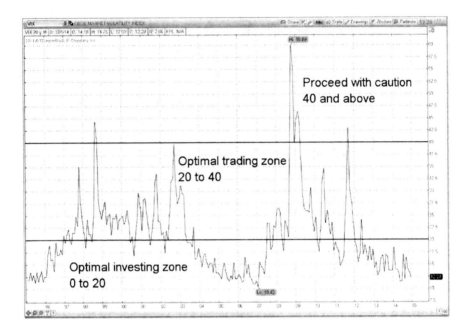

Figure 50 shows a monthly closing price chart of the VIX, highlighting the best course of action for each zone.

Figure 51 shows a daily chart of the VIX with the price of the S&P 500 on top. As you can see, the last three tests of the 20 level pivot on the VIX have made for great buying opportunities. This will not always be the case as time goes on. Eventually, the VIX will get back above 20 again.

This example is intended to show you how to train your mind to look for these types of patterns to give yourself an added edge, while also keeping in mind that these patterns do eventually get broken.

Figure 51: VIX with S&P chart on top

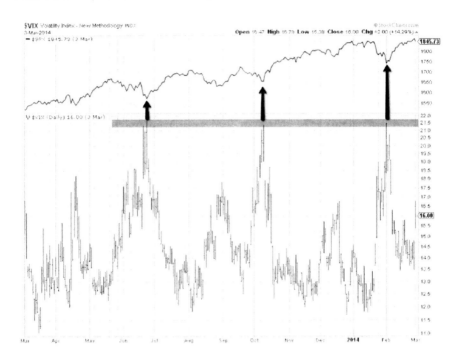

SWING TRADING PLAYBOOK IN PRACTICE

I will now put together all of the topics I have covered in this section on swing trading in some real-world examples. Here I will show a series of charts and walk through the market analysis using the topics we have discussed to illustrate how one could have traded these situations most effectively.

Example 1: S&P 500 Index

In this first example, I am using the weekly chart of the S&P 500 Index. Figure 52 shows the macro picture going back to the origin of the bull market in 2009. As the example proceeds, I will take sections of this chart and drill down for a closer look and go step-by-step through the process. To begin, let's observe the macro picture.

Figure 52: Weekly S&P 500 since 2009

We see back in the fall of 2008 a failed rally attempt that wasn't able to produce a higher high on the price chart, nor to get back above the midpoint of the previous decline. That established the next short setup lower through early 2009. At this time, we began to see noticeable bullish divergences in the NYSE cumulative advance-decline line.

Eventually buyers stepped in and were able to break the downside momentum by pushing prices higher than the previous failed rally attempt and also above the midpoint of the last sell-off. Price then produced the first higher high on the weekly bar chart since the financial crisis of 2007-08 began.

Once the last major high was taken out, the sellers came out again and a sell-off began that took the form of an A-B-C style correction into support below. Once support was established, the rally continued to its first measured move upside target. This target is obtained by measuring the length of the first rally and adding it to the correction's low price.

Once that target was achieved, there was another retracement, eventually matching the size of the previous correction in percentage terms before finding support below. The market continued its upward trajectory into the next upside target, which was obtained by using the box theory method, where you would add the size of the last rally to the high of the previous rally to come up with a logical target.

The box theory target ended up doing a good job of providing resistance to the market average and it resulted in the biggest correction since the 2009 market lows were established. Price then continued to progress higher, hitting a few more measured move targets and a box theory target along the way to the point at the end of the chart.

I know this may be a lot to comprehend at once, so let's now break this down step-by-step to shed more light on what was happening.

Figure 53: S&P 500

The first part is to attempt to identify the trend change. Referring to Figure 53, the last failed rally attempt in the fall of 2008 brought the S&P 500 up 202 points from high to low. The rally off the March 2009 lows eventually halted around the 868 price level. If you add the 202 points of the previous rally to the 666 intraday low of March 2009, it yields the 868 price level.

The market paused briefly and continued higher, eventually taking out the high of the previous failed rally attempt. Also, remember the NYSE cumulative advance-decline line was showing bullish divergences during the early 2009 sell-off (which gives the attempted upside breakout even more credence).

Let's now assume the trend had reversed upwards given this recent market data and let's also assume you hadn't yet taken any swing long positions because of the ferocity of the recent sell-off that was still clear in your mind. At this point, it would be extremely hard to buy a new recent high when it's a short time horizon. It would have been wise to stick to day trading until a pullback presented itself.

Fortunately, in this case we got a pullback not long after the previous highs were breached. This produced an A-B-C style correction that resulted in a third and final wave that found support with confluence next to a prior swing high (the horizontal line to the right-hand side of the chart).

At this point you had two options: just go for it by taking the trade when support is reached, or you could wait for the first buy signal after support is reached and place your stop below the swing low left behind. In this case, either method would have worked just fine. As you can see on the far right of the chart, the first daily close above the previous daily high became an ideal entry point as the market continued higher and never looked back.

We need a target, so we go to our measured moves concept to come up with a logical upside target by taking the most recent price action into account. So in this case, we would measure from the March 2009 closing lows to the highest close before the A-B-C correction (along with the intraday high and lows) and add that to the swing low of the A-B-C correction.

We have a closing low at 676.53 and a closing high at 946.21, which equates to about 270 points. We can then add that 270 points to the low of the A-B-C correction, which was 869.32, to come up with our first upside target at 1139 on the S&P 500.

The next steps are illustrated in Figure 54. Here we see the buy signal for those who waited for it. The measured move target came in at 1139 and was achieved in the beginning of the year 2010. Measured move and box theory targets are meant to give you a place to take profits and establish a risk versus reward picture. As you see, they can also be places where the market has a chance to reverse trend in some way.

In this example, once the measured move target at 1139 was achieved, it kicked off another correction which equalled the size in percentage terms (9%) of the previous correction experienced during the A-B-C correction.

Figure 54: S&P 500

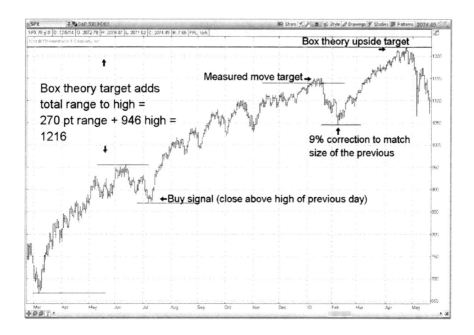

If you had taken profits or sold out completely at the measured move target, you could have chosen that spot to buy back once again. This time the first upside target would be found using the box theory method. So in this case, we would then add the 270 point range to the high of the first rally off the March 2009 lows.

This would equate to approximately 1216 on the S&P 500, which is not as attractive in terms of risk-to-reward as the prior swing long trade, but it is still attractive enough to take the entry. Again, one could have taken the swing long trade as soon as prices traded, or waited for a buy signal to follow. The result was another successful trade.

The next thing we see is the target for that last long trade became strong resistance for a correction that started with a flash crash and ended in an A-B-C correction pattern (see Figure 55).

Figure 55: S&P 500

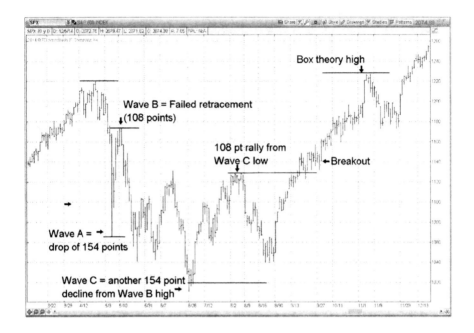

Referring to Figure 55, wave A was a *doozy*, a *fat finger* crash of the US stock market that took all of about 60 minutes and terrified everyone that wasn't short. At this point, wave A was obviously the biggest reaction against the trend that had been experienced since the March 2009 lows. This takes us back to the rule of thumb on A-B-C corrections. When the initial wave of selling is greater than anything experienced in recent history, it usually results in another wave of equal selling before any type of a bottom can be anticipated.

This particular wave A took the S&P 500 down 154 points from high to low. The retracement wave B was 108 points before the failure (a close below the low of the prior day). Then we have wave C, which became another approximately 154 point decline from the wave B high. This also coincided with the 38% retracement level of the entire rally off the 2009 lows. This came into play during the 2011 correction as well, as we will see in just a moment.

After the wave C low, the market attempted another rally that stalled when the size of the rally off its low price stretched to about 108 points, matching the size of the failed retracement in wave B. At this point, the trend still had not flipped upward. For all we knew at this time, the market could roll over once more.

However, this time the market found support at a higher low and shortly thereafter took out the last swing high and continued to stretch its rally size to greater than that experienced in wave B. It was at this point that the trend had turned upward and the first upside target would be in the form of the box theory method. We would add the 108 point trading range to the high that was broken out from. This gave us our next upside target in the 1230 area on the S&P 500.

Figure 56: S&P 500

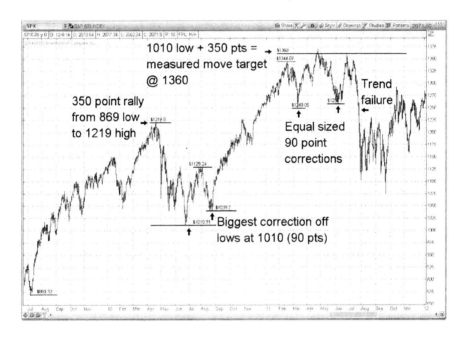

In the next chart, Figure 56, we can see the box theory target was achieved and the market continued moving higher. At this point, we would have looked for the full measured move target by using recent history as our guide. The most recent rally produced a 350 point advance from high to low. We would have then added that to our low at 1010 to come up with a measured move target for swing longs around 1360 on the S&P 500.

Now let's look at the micro moves in between the swing highs and lows. There were certainly opportunities for shorter-term swing traders using the same methods. In terms of longer-term swing trades and analysing markets and the trend, you need to stay aware of the supply and demand patterns of the market. Even on the micro level, you need to gauge what is in line with the trend and what is out of line and a signal of caution.

I have marked on Figure 57 the first correction inside this macro move off the lows at 1010. It proved to be about 90 points in length. Once price got above 1300, there were two of these similar sized corrections in a short time span. The problem was, the market then failed to make any more upside progress after support was found. Eventually a new lower low was created and so the pattern that had been in place since the lows at 1010 was broken. This was a clear indication that something more to the downside was in the works, as buyers weren't able to keep the momentum going.

I have talked about using upside targets as potential resistance. I am not in favour of blindly shorting when upside targets are reached, since it's clearly not aligning yourself with the dominant trend and it then takes an awful lot of skill and mental fortitude to hold such a position. I am, however, in favour of taking a counter trend trade at target areas after a signal has occurred.

So, for this example, if you wanted to get short at the measured move target, you should have waited for a close below the low of the previous day. You could have then taken your shot with a stop above the swing high left behind. There were a couple of opportunities in this example that would have been successful – you can see in the chart two occasions where price got to the measured move target and then pulled back. The first time, the price overshot the measured move target but pulled back and turned into a minor correction. The second time, the price retraced to very close to the measured move target before it pulled back again.

Figure 57: S&P 500

I talked above about the significance of 38% retracement levels in a macro bull market. While the market doesn't always stop on a dime at these levels, as in Figure 57, history has shown it's best to stay on the right side of this price level in the long term.

We see both the 2010 and 2011 corrections end at or near their 38% retracement level. When you see a counter trend reaction that is greater than any in recent history, look for your 38% retrace level and match it up with a previous significant high or an A-B-C correction pattern projection to look for potential support.

We now move on to Figure 58. Once the market found support at the 38% retracement, there was a breakout above the previous high and a larger retracement rally than the one previous. This meant odds favoured that the breakout was for real. The market dropped 10% after the breakout, which matched the size of the last minor drop to the 1074 lows.

Figure 58: S&P 500

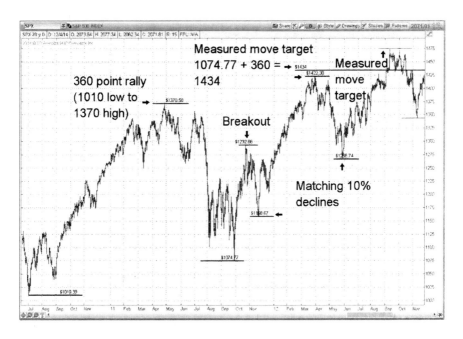

Having determined that a trend change has occurred, the next target became a measured move upside projection. We would have added the length of the previous rally (360 points) to the most current low at 1074 to get a target of approximately 1434.

That high wasn't quite hit at the first attempt, but very close, before there was another correction of 10%, matching the size of the previous and lining up with the swing high of the breakout at 1292, as support. It was not long until price then achieved the measured move upside target and moved higher.

The next eventual swing high became a different sort of measured move on the macro level. This kicked off another similar style correction of about 130 points. At the time of writing, the market continues to grind higher and higher in a series of micro measured moves. There is no telling just how high the major averages will go before a meaningful correction kicks in.

The most important thing is to continue to align yourself with the current trends of the market. Until there is a correction of greater than 10% (which is the largest experienced since the 2011 lows), there isn't any real reason to play the hero and attempt to call the top.

Before I conclude this example, I will show you what the *other* measured move target turned out to be. In Figure 59 of the S&P 500, you see during the 2002 to 2007 bull market the price of the S&P 500 advanced 807 points from low to high. When you added that same amount to the lows of March 2009, it equated to 1474 on the S&P 500. I really don't think it's a coincidence that the market stopped there, although briefly.

These patterns are available everywhere, it just takes some time to know what to look for and how to take the right course of action with the information in real time. This, in my opinion, works far better than any new trading fad, headline news and opinions, or whatever else you can think of. Just spot the patterns and align yourself with the trends until they fail. Put the blinders on regarding everything else.

Towards the end of the chart, the market had pushed well past the 1474 high. From a macro perspective it tells me this bull market is for real and here to stay. That doesn't mean it will not be a volatile ride up, but it does tell me that the overall trajectory is higher.

Figure 59: S&P 500

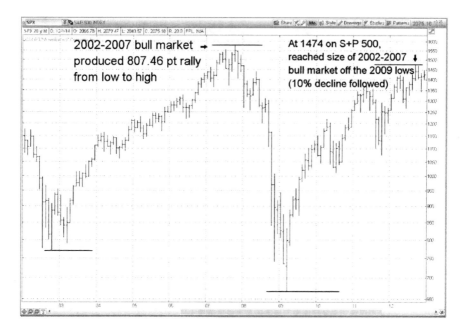

Example 2: The NASDAQ 100 ETF (QQQ)

In this second example, we will look at a long-term chart of the ETF of another major market average, the NASDAQ 100. The ticker symbol for this exchange traded fund is QQQ. This index is comprised of 100 of the largest companies, mostly in the technology sector, by market cap. Examples include Amazon, Microsoft, Apple, Google and Intel.

As you can see on the weekly chart in Figure 60, many of the setups were similar to those of the S&P 500 in the previous example. First there was an initial breakout, followed by an A-B-C correction. The market found support and continued higher into the first measured move target. That target proved to be resistance, as well, and it produced a correction that matched the size of the previous one by percentage. Eventually, the market found support once again and it was followed by another rally higher into the next target above, which was the box theory target.

It was here that things differentiated from the S&P 500 and at this point I will delve into the chart in more detail.

Figure 60: Weekly chart of QQQ

We can take a closer look at the price action in the daily chart in Figure 61. We can see the initial breakout which took the QQQ's up about $12 from low to high. This calculation gave a measured move target for the next rally higher that followed the A-B-C correction. A maximum upside target was given by the box theory, where the $12 measured move would be added to the high of the range. This level then becomes resistance in the process.

Figure 61: Closer look at QQQ price action

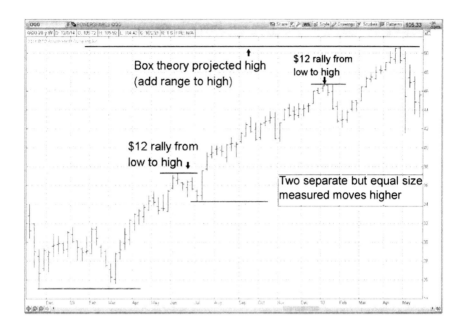

We fast forward to the next sequence of events that took place – see Figure 62 – and we can see a distinct correction pattern in the QQQ's of approximately $9 in each occurrence. In each case, the retracements found support at or near the previous swing highs, so the confluence of previous swing highs and the repeated pattern of same size corrections made for some excellent longer-term swing trading opportunities.

Figure 62: QQQ

The first measured move target shown in Figure 63 was calculated by adding the length of the previous rally to the swing low that formed – in this case that meant adding the rally of $18 to the low at $49.93 to give approximately $68. That target was achieved and then briefly breached before another $9 correction took hold in late 2012.

Figure 63: QQQ

Let's also look at another confluence area for resistance. Remember the higher high patterns that can often develop. It's always a good idea to identify higher highs in an uptrend and lower lows in a downtrend. They can contribute added weight to a support or resistance level and they can also give you a clue as to whether the current trend is slowing or strengthening.

In Figure 63, we can see how the $68 area on the QQQ had added resistance confluence. By gauging the price levels of the higher highs it was possible to identify a target level (measured move upside) that coincided with the next projected higher high.

In these cases where there are multiple confluences, it is extremely important to pay close attention to the signals the market generates around them. In this case it was wise to take profits ahead of the $68 level because the chances of it proving to be a viable target and also a resistance level were increased by the confluence of factors.

I will finish this example by highlighting where the market found support. In Figure 64, I have removed all drawings and just highlighted the support levels. Again you can see where each correction stopped – in each case it occurred at or near to the prior swing high on the chart.

Figure 64: QQQ

I think traditional technical analysis has it all wrong. Most tend to focus on previous swing lows in an uptrend and great weight is attached to this. "If the market takes out the previous low, then look out," is what you hear from many technicians.

However, in most cases the real support comes from the prior swing highs in the uptrend. I encourage you to look at your price charts and mark off the prior highs that have been left behind in the uptrend, and in a downtrend look for the prior swing lows.

Use the tools you've learned to measure the supply and demand imbalances and try to line up your projected levels with a nearby pivot for added confluence. Then go for it!

Let's look at some more examples.

Example 3: SPDR Gold Trust ETF (GLD)

For the next example, I will discuss an asset class in a technical downtrend for a change of pace. I will use the most popular ETF for gold (ticker symbol:GLD). Figure 65 shows the macro picture of this investment vehicle.

Figure 65: SPDR Gold Trust ETF (GLD)

After the correction during the 2008 financial crisis, gold continued its long-term uptrend and relative outperformance. Three years later, during another panic-driven event – this time originating in Europe – gold prices topped out and went into a near-term downtrend.

The initial wave of selling took place in late 2011 and that took the price of GLD down a nearly identical amount as the last major correction in 2008. The retracement failed and price fell to another lower low, achieving its measured move downside target and box theory target.

Towards the right-hand side of the chart gold prices consolidated near the box theory downside target and where the correction in progress matched the 2008 correction in terms of percentages. Up to the point where the chart ends a retracement rally had failed, but the market had struggled with the $120 price level. Let's take a closer look at the downtrend.

Figure 66: SPDR Gold Trust ETF (GLD)

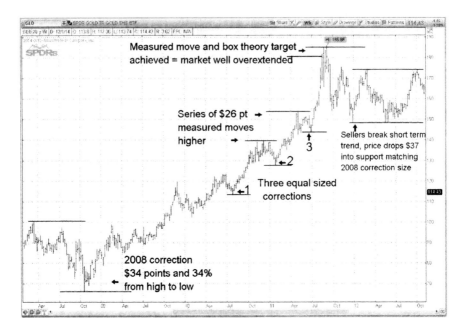

In Figure 66 we see the 2008 correction once again, which dropped the price of GLD down $34 and 34%. As the uptrend continued in a series of micro measured moves long, the pattern began to get a bit stretched. I've highlighted the last series of micro measured moves higher. They consisted of $26 advances followed by $12 declines.

Later on in 2011 as the euro zone crisis emerged, the buying of gold accelerated. The last push higher saw the measured move target and the box theory target (by adding the $26 point advances to the high) achieved without any real retracement. When this happens the market is overextended. This doesn't mean that the price can't continue higher, it simply means that any new positions established at that point would be extremely risky.

Soon after the swift advance, the first short-term upside trend break occurred as the $12 decline pattern in the uptrend was clearly broken. This is not surprising to see in an overly extended market and, needless to say, the sell-off gained momentum shortly thereafter. As prices fell, it was then time to look for confluence to determine where support might be established.

In this case, there was a confluence zone that consisted of the prior swing high (horizontal line) that coincided with a $34 point drop from highs – this would match the length of the 2008 correction. The combination of these factors made it likely that this would become support on the pullback, at least on the first test.

Figure 67: SPDR Gold Trust ETF (GLD)

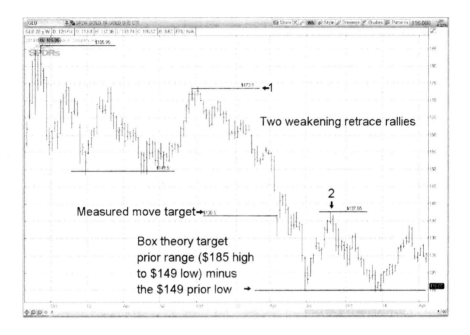

Figure 67 provides a detailed look at the correction using a close only line chart. Again we see the initial drop into support that followed with three separate, but similar sized, retracement rallies that could not seem to make a whole lot of progress overall. After the third failed attempt to break resistance, gold continued its descent below $150.

That break down was greeted with additional selling activity, now that the size of the 2008 correction had been exceeded. Our first measured move target below was in the $138.50 range, which was achieved and exceeded without much of a fight from the buyers. The next logical downside target became the projected low of the next trading range from the box theory method. This came in around $114.50 and when price approached this level it provided some short-term support for gold prices.

If I was trading onwards from the point where this example ends, I would like to see these retracement rallies strengthen in size before we can even begin to think about calling a bottom. Unfortunately, the rallies seemed to be weakening, as the last retracement rally took prices up $11 from low to high on a closing basis. This failed to even match the size of the previous retracement rally off the support zone at $149.50 (which was approximately $14 points). The drop to this support zone from the highs equated to an approximate 38% correction, which matched the size of the 2008 correction in terms of percentages.

At the time of writing, gold prices continued to consolidate inside the lower end of this most recent range. In terms of risk-to-reward, the swing trade longs tended to have the upper hand, but they would have to defend the support levels that they have created.

Example 4: Interest rates and bond prices (TNX and TLT)

This next example is based on a pair of blog posts I wrote in July and August 2013.

At the time I created this example there had been a lot of chatter regarding interest rates, so I wanted to take some time to look at the technicals along with the supply and demand patterns. US interest rates had moved considerably higher over a period of a few months, which had led many to believe this environment was here to stay.

In Figure 68, we are following ticker symbol TNX, which tracks the yield or interest rate of 10 year Treasury bonds, which is thought to be the benchmark of interest rates. This is a monthly chart going all the way back to 1998. On the chart I have highlighted two significant bear markets. I have also highlighted three significant bull markets by marking the low to highs with horizontal lines and also adding annotations.

Let's walk through some of the characteristics of this price action, from left to right.

There was a bear market correction of 39 points (or 3.90%) from high to low. A bull market then pushed rates back up into the midpoint (marked with a horizontal line) of the prior trading range. The following bear market saw interest rates decrease another 3.9% (39 points), which matched the previous decline. At that point the technical signs seemed to point to interest rates rising to at least retest the midpoint (at 3.35%) of the most recent trading range, just as they did from 2003 to 2007.

Figure 68: Weekly chart of TNX

Another thing we should take away from this is the fact that rates rose almost the entire time of the 2002 to 2007 bull market in equities. I think there is a consensus building among commentators that rising interest rates could be crippling for the stock market. Maybe a parabolic move in interest rates would indeed be damaging, but a gradual rise in rates due to increased anticipation of real economic growth, in my opinion, wouldn't be harmful.

We then move on to Figure 69, which is a weekly chart of interest rates showing short-term support and resistance. Downside support should come in around the 2.30% area. If rates can break above the 2.75% to 2.85% area, I would expect that retest of the trading range midpoint at 3.35% I referred to before. This would also match the size of the last bull market in interest rates.

The last three bull markets in rates over the past 15 years have produced moves of 2.0%, 2.2% and 2.7% higher. I don't think we should expect anything less from this one.

Figure 69: Weekly chart of TNX

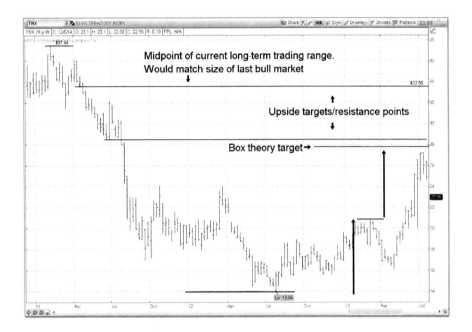

Figure 70 shows the weekly price action in TLT, or the long-term US Treasury ETF, going all the way back to 2009. Bond prices and interest rates move inversely – as rates rise, the prices of bonds drop, and vice versa. The bonds with the highest durations or longest date to maturity usually get hit the hardest when rates rise.

Bonds become cheaper when interest rates rise because, for example, if rates were to move to 4.0%, all of a sudden a bond paying 2.0% will be less sought after. Less demand for these bonds decreases their value and price.

In the chart of TLT we can see the bear market that long-term treasuries endured from the end of 2008 until 2010. I've annotated the setup in TLT at the time of this chart – there had been matching 17 point corrections from high to low. Support had been found at the $106.50 level and resistance stood at $114 to $116.

Figure 70: US Treasury ETF (TLT)

I believe eventually TLT should go on to test the downside support levels marked on the chart, which would match the size of the last significant bear market and also retest the breakout point in 2011. This area should become strong support for a move higher. At this point it was too soon to tell if we would ever see new highs again, but I think these support levels would be a good spot to step in if you were looking for some bond exposure.

Lastly, let's take a look at the 10 year Treasury interest rates once again (see Figure 71). I have highlighted on the chart how interest rates moved during each of the Federal Reserve's Quantitative Easing programmes. QE 1+2 produced a 1.41-1.55 basis point rise in yields. Please note that the figures in the chart are 10 times the actual interest rate. So 22.92 is a 2.292% interest rate.

Once interest rates rose to the $28-29.50 levels (horizontal lines on the far right of the chart), it effectively matched the size of the previous rises in interest rates in term of basis points. It was likely the next short-term move would be to the downside, which inversely would be good for bonds. As the US economy continued to improve and investors became more willing to hold risky assets, as opposed to cash, I would expect interest rates to make their way to the next upside target around 3.37%.

It is worth noting that although rates at this point had matched the size of the previous moves higher in terms of basis points, in terms of percentage moves this move higher was larger, basically doubling off the all-time lows.

Figure 71: TNX

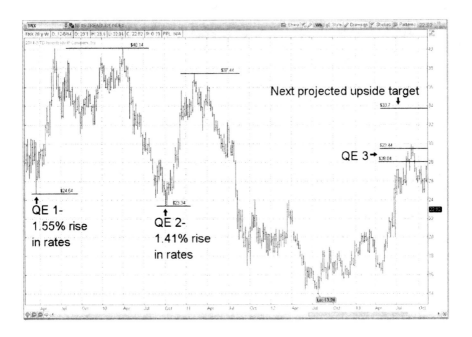

*   *   *

I used this example to make a point. While many, if not most, were looking for higher rates in 2014, I used some of these analysis methods to challenge the overall theme of how high rates would go.

This goes to show that analysis of supply and demand can sometimes show you things that fundamental analysis might not be able to in the short term.

Example 5: Historical Dow Jones Industrial Average

I will no doubt get reactions to the methods in this book that say these patterns are some new phenomenon due to the recent rise of robot trading. So I have decided to conclude with a pattern on the historical chart of the Dow Jones Industrial Average (DJIA).

Figure 72: DJIA since the 1920s

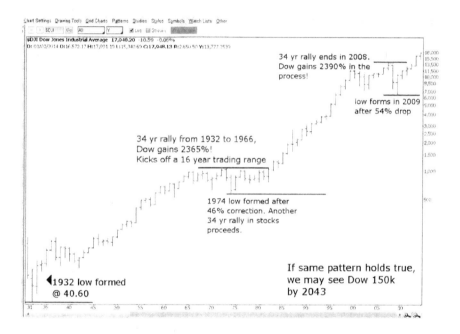

Figure 72 goes back to the 1920s. It shows that the macro bull market took the Dow up from 40.60 in 1932 to 1000 by the 1960s – a percentage gain of approximately 2365%. This matched the size of the macro bull market that began at the lows of 1974 and rose to the highs of 2007 (or 2000) by producing gains also just over 2300%.

That means if the pattern holds we could be looking at Dow 150,000 by the year 2043! Obviously this is a long way off and it is not meant to be a prediction. This is simply to show you that although previous market patterns do not repeat, they often rhyme.

Let's take a look at another historical pattern.

Figure 73: Monthly chart of the DJIA from 1965

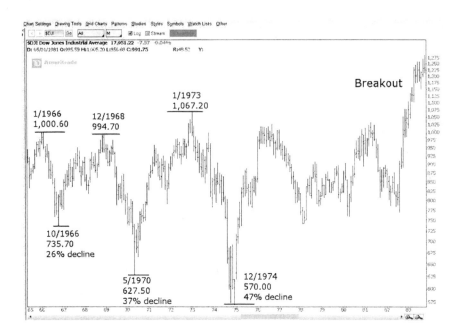

I thought it would also be interesting to take some time to dissect some of the price action that occurred during the last long-term trading range in the major averages, and then compare that price action to the long-term trading range from 2000-2012, which was broken out of in 2012.

Figure 73 is a monthly chart of the Dow Jones Industrial Average during the major long-term trading range that began in 1966. I have highlighted the three highs on the chart along with the price level and date they occurred. I have also highlighted the price level of the three lower lows, and the date and size of the decline.

Note that once the third lower low was formed in 1974 after a 47% decline in the average, a bull market emerged that took the Dow to a new all-time high. Although there were bear markets along the way, like in 1987, the major averages never really looked back.

Now let's fast forward to the present. We see a very similar pattern of higher highs and lower lows, even the correction sizes roughly equal out as well.

Figure 74: Monthly chart of the DJIA from 1997

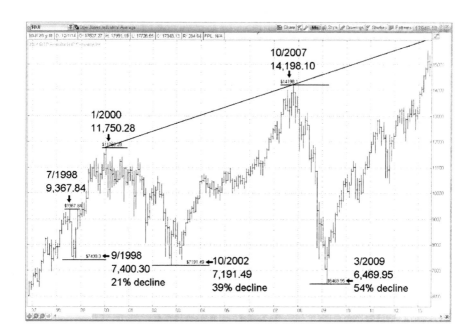

Figure 74 is also a monthly chart of the Dow Jones Industrial Average. It shows the price action during the long-term trading range from the 1998 bull market high to the 2007 bull market high, and the breakout to the upside in 2012-2013. As before, I have highlighted the price level of the three higher highs, along with dates, as well as the three price levels of the lower lows, along with the dates and the size of the declines.

Let's take a look at the similarities. First off, we have a similar pattern of three lower lows, each producing bigger drops than the previous. Notice also the similarities in the size of the declines in terms of percentage. The 1966 to 1982 trading range produces three drops of 26%, 37% and 47% respectively. The 1998 to 2013 trading range produced three drops of 21%, 39% and 54% respectively.

If you recall, during the 1966 to 1982 trading range, the third low was the final low before the real breakout. Now we find ourselves in a similar predicament, where our third low produced back in 2009 has been followed by a legitimate breakout to new all-time highs on both the Dow and the S&P 500.

Will it hold?

Only time will tell if the rise will continue, but it seems to me that it would not make a whole lot of sense to fight against this bull trend until/unless sellers and bears can prove themselves. One way they can do that is to push prices back into the long-term trading range below the 2007 bull market high that came in around 14,200. Until then, it's probably best to give the upside the benefit of the doubt.

That concludes the swing trading playbook.

Additional Trading Tips

Trading is a difficult endeavour. The learning curve lasts years and it can take a lot out of you both emotionally and monetarily in the process. I've read statistics that say over 90% of traders fail and give up. I have no way to know for sure if that statistic is accurate or not. Even in the case where that failure rate is accurate, I still believe that with a sound strategy and risk management plan, anyone can beat the odds.

My hope is that the knowledge I share in this book can help shorten the learning curve for those new to trading, and help give some new ideas to those who are more experienced at trading but seeking to learn more.

I'll end with a few other ideas that helped me on my learning curve.

Start a blog

Keep track of your thoughts in an easily managed and accessible location. Most blogs give you the option to remain hidden from everyone except those who you designate, if you prefer to stay anonymous. Or if you want to share with the world and possibly make some new connections with others in the trading community, you can easily do that too.

Create a post early in the morning outlining some of your expectations and game plan. Come up with a few different scenarios to prepare for, based upon where the market opens. Then create a post after the trading day to capture your thoughts on how the day went according to your plan (or how far it differed from your plan).

This way you will get a macro picture of your strategy and see if there are any weaknesses you need to work on and strengths that you can build upon. Committing to do this each day will help your discipline as well.

Keep track of all your trades

There are many great resources out there that will take account of all your trades, so that you can run all sorts of statistical analysis on them. This will further help you to define your strengths and weaknesses.

These tools are generally provided with most popular trading platforms, such as Investor R/T (www.linnsoft.com), NinjaTrader (www.ninjatrader.com) and S5 trader from Stage 5 Trading (www.stage5trading.com). My personal favourite is StockTickr (www.stocktickr.com) and Trading Journal Spreadsheet (trading-journal-spreadsheet.com) is good too.

You may find that you need to make adjustments to your risk management strategy, or that you don't have a lot of success during trend days. Whatever the outcome, you won't truly know for sure if you don't keep good records of all your trades and thought processes.

Filter your financial media consumption

By the time macro events hit the headlines of news stations, they have mostly been priced into the market. Too much financial media consumption when you are day trading can begin to ingrain personal biases in you, whether consciously or not. That goes for websites as well as TV stations. Actually, certain websites can be devastating for your trading.

You should enter the day with a completely open mind and anything which distracts you from achieving this should be discarded immediately. If you want to watch that TV show or visit that website or chat room, do it after the market is closed, not during or right before the trading day.

I remember early on in my trading having the TV running in the background along with 10 to 15 blogs and financial websites going, and refreshing them every 15 minutes or so to read the updates and all the comments. I wondered why I was so erratic with my trading execution. I was suffering from paralysis from over analysis. I was consuming too much media at once.

It wasn't until I let all that go and added a true game plan and strategy that I saw my trading results improve.

Having said that, you don't want to be oblivious to financial news either, which leads me to my final point.

Keep track of what's coming up on the economic calendar

You can find an economic calendar from many different sources, such as Forex Factory (www.forexfactory.com), Briefing (www.briefing.com) and the *Wall Street Journal* (www.wsj.com), to name a few.

Make sure you know what times that major economic news will be released. So if there is a major economic data point being released at 10 am EST, you probably don't want to take your initial entry point right at 9:59 am. If the Federal Reserve is releasing its FOMC statement, you probably don't want to put on a trade right before the release of that either.

One way around this is to subscribe to Trade the News (www.tradethenews.com) or Trade the Markets (www.tradethemarkets.com) type service and tune in around the time the economic numbers are being released. Another alternative is to open the economic calendar site of your choice and refresh it until you get the results.

Whatever you decide, just make sure you know when the major economic news items are being released and plan accordingly.

Conclusion

I will go back to what I said initially in the Preface. When I began to throw aside all of the weight of others' opinions, predictions, lagging indicators, etc., and focus squarely on price action alone, my trading began to be consistently successful. And that is one of my main objectives in writing this book. I wanted to offer some fresh new ideas to the trading community.

I know this is not what one usually finds in a book regarding trading and technical analysis. There were no trend lines, no head and shoulders patterns, and no RSIs and MACD waiting for confirmation. That's because I have never found any of that traditional technical analysis helpful in the least bit.

Some of you may have been turned off by the simplistic approach. After all, you can't be successful at something so difficult as trading by adding and subtracting a few highs and lows, can you? To those of you thinking this way, I say just give it a try. Try it out in a simulation account. What do you have to lose?

Most of all, thanks for taking the time to read this book. I am most appreciative and I hope you found it helpful. Please feel free to contact me at any time using the email address at the start of the book.

Best of luck in all of your trading!

Glossary of Terms

Fade (or fading the market) – Taking a position that goes counter to the primary trend of the market. Traders fade market moves because the majority of gains are usually seen in the first part of the move, when everyone else is trying to chase the performance. Fading the market, if done properly, can prove extremely profitable.

Fading the gap – To trade in the opposite direction of the opening gap in expectation of a gap fill. So if the gap is 1900 and the market gaps up by opening at 1905, fading the gap would essentially mean taking a short trade in the expectation of price trading back down to 1900 to fill that gap. And vice versa for gap downs.

Gap fill – When gaps are filled within the same trading day on which they occur.

Globex (overnight session) – An electronic trading platform used for derivatives, futures and commodity contracts. Globex runs continuously, so it is not restricted by borders or time zones. In this book's examples, Globex specifically refers to the hours that the regular stock market is closed.

Inside day – A day in which the total range of prices is within the previous day's price range.

Light (as in shorts should be light) – Referring to position size. If a trade is a high probability but counter trend, generally the position size should be smaller than normal, or light.

Long (as in long the market) – The buying of a security such as a stock, commodity or currency, with the expectation that the asset's price will rise.

Opening swing – The price which a particular security opens the trading day at.

Pit session – Otherwise known as the regular trading hours session (RTH) for US stocks and securities. It is the 9:30 am EST open to the 4:15pm EST close.

Pivots – Specific price levels where prices have reversed in the past.

Scalper – A very short-term trader only looking to trade for ticks (or quarter points) at a time.

Settlement price – Also known as closing price. The last traded price level before the close of the RTH session.

Short (as in short the market) – When one borrows or sells to open a position in the belief that the security is overpriced and headed lower. The borrower must eventually buy back the security (hopefully at a lower price than they sold it for) to close the transaction.

Trend day – When the market opens in one direction and proceeds in that direction the entire day without a gap fill. Generally you get an unusually large gap up or down, maybe on some economic number or central bank statement, etc. Then price continues in the same direction throughout the day with very little retracement.

Whipsaw – Sharp price movements up and down inside a narrow range, which can cause traders to overtrade and lose money easily.

Add to your technical analysis library

TRAMLINE TRADING

A practical guide to swing trading with tramlines,
Elliott Waves and Fibonacci levels

By John Burford

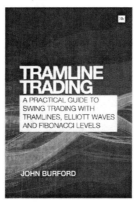

A straightforward, winning trading method

There are certain universal chart patterns that are traced out time and
time again by markets - these patterns have stood the test of time and
can be instantly recognised by a skilled trader. When you learn how
to spot these patterns and use them to forecast market action you
have the basis of a winning trading method. Tramline Trading is a
complete practical guide that shows you precisely how to do this.

The Tramline Trading Method described here is a simple and complete
system which combines Fibonacci levels, basic Elliott Wave Theory and
John Burford's original tramline concepts. It is based on a small number
of highly reliable patterns and can be put to use in any market. Every
detail of how to put the method into practice is revealed, including
how to spot developing patterns for high-probability, low-risk trades,
where to place entry orders and stop losses, and the five best setups to
look out for. Full colour chart illustrations are used throughout.

If you are looking for a proven trading method that is reliable and
easy to execute then Tramline Trading will put you on the right track.
It is the essential new guide to a winning trading approach.

CPSIA information can be obtained at www.ICGtesting.com
Printed in the USA
LVOW07s1704231015

459499LV00007B/85/P